THE
QUEEN OF
CHINA
AND
OTHER POEMS
BY
EDWARD
SHANKS

LONDON
MARTIN SECKER
MCMXIX

TO

NAOMI ROYDE-SMITH

THIS BOOK IS AFFECTIONATELY

AND GRATEFULLY DEDICATED

I am indebted to the Editors of The New Statesman, To-Day *and* The Westminster Gazette, *in whose pages many of these pieces first appeared.*

E. S.

CONTENTS

THE COMPLAINTS

THE COMPLAINTS

To H. C. Harwood

I

WELL, I am tired at last ! I put away
Languor and lassitude and all regrets.
Better, I said, the dull but solid day
Than an endless reckoning of hopeless debts,
Unheard complaints, unanswered prayers, unseen
Genuflexions to an unbelieved in God.
But I am not so dull as I have been ;
Too long this long and lightless way I have trod
And suddenly now I see what thing I tread,
Lit by a transient flash of the lightning brain,
That leaps in the sky an instant and is dead
But, having shown, needs not to come again.
Ridiculous treadmill ! that the sorry fool
Thinks is the road to joy, his brain is so dull.

II

You, to whom Heaven gave all the gifts I need,
Money and leisure, long I followed you

And made the lightest line you wrote my creed
And gave you the extravagant praise I thought was due.
I'd sneer at you now, to pay my less lucky case,
For sneering is easy from the poor to the rich,
Throw witty songs in your cold and happy face
And ease on your books the beggar's endless itch.
But still from your heaven of unmoved success,
You cast your gifts to me for my delight,
You from your wealth to me in wretchedness,
And every gift of yours in my eyes is bright.
Strange power, strange happiness, strange poetry!
That even envy cannot twist awry.

III

There are many countries that I have not seen,
And many kinds of men I have not met,
But all the gracious towns where I have been
Haunt in my brain and whisper there and set
Strange echoes going with their lovely names,
Birdlip and Paris, Fontainebleau and Wells,
Places that live in me like happy dreams
And sound in the present day like distant bells.
Here I am set and there's no end, no end;
Too soon the vision closes, too long remains,
Like the last long talk one had with a lost friend,
Whose memory lingers on, when friendship wanes.

Better to stay at home! The towns one sees
Trammel the day with stupid memories.

IV

I was a soldier once. How fear was then
Mixed with bright honour and delightful pride!
How different we were from other men,
Who lived in houses and in houses died!
How huge the morning was, before the sun
Sullenly found us marching in the mist!
And sleep was dark and deep when work was done
And food awoke in us a greedy zest.
But all that's over. I no more shall see,
Quick to the word and ready to my hand,
The smooth and easy moving company
Marching in column on the heathery land.
There's no pride now and fear's the fear that's bred
Of money and suchlike maggots in the head.

V

THE EMPTY HOUSE, i

We walked all morning over furze and grass,
And climbed steep tufted heights against the sun,
Went down the shaven tracks, where rabbits pass,
And unalarmed the scuttling pheasants run.

5

There were no men in sight, save at a farm,
Where, far below, we saw, about midday,
Two ploughmen lying lapped about with warm
Rank growings of the hedge. Green buds of may
Hung over them unopened, primroses
Were yellow round their bodies. On we went,
Up a long slope through tangled coppices,
Where half-fledged hazels on the pathway leant,
Till suddenly we saw through thinning boughs
The chimneys of an old long-lonely house.

VI

THE EMPTY HOUSE, ii

The door was gone, the jambs aslant, awry,
The roof grown over with the mosses slow,
The windows stared with blank and empty eye,
Half the panes gone. The flagstones grinned below
In gaping cracks. The foolish cattle came
About the orchard, where the unpruned trees
Held to the sky white boughs of trembling flame,
And long wild grasses brushed about our knees.
The dumb house called to us, the black, wide door
Stood open for us long and stood in vain :
Sighing we guessed those old walls held a store
Of rest for us when we should come again

6

Into the hollow, long and green and still—
Then turned away to cross the further hill.

VII

I sat once in the curved arm of a tree
Over the salty marsh, above the wide
And misty mere, half river and half sea,
Where faint low hills marked out the further side.
Then time passed over as I bade it go,
Fast when in joy my hurrying heart beat fast,
And when sweet rest inhabited me, so slow
I did not know if a day or an hour had passed.
Thus I retarded or advanced the day,
That subject and sweet minion of my will,
But now with stubborn beats the hours go their way
Like clouds in a steady wind and new hours still
Loom up behind them and heavily go by
In the same swift and daunting monotony.

VIII

I am sick of devices and of policies,
Of the restless nerves, of the itches, aches and strains,
And the tiresome long pursuit that balances
My sluggish brain against their stupid brains.
Oh, under beauty's whip I still can run

7

And match my pace against another's pace';
I only ask a little air and the sun
Falling in warmth upon my upward face.
But these dull rains of weather and the mind
Shut the world from me in a sombre veil
And memories of old weariness lie behind
And hours to be, ill-nourished, clammy, pale,
Lie on my forward journey and fill the way,
As the dull day fades into a new dull day.

IX

When in the mines of dark and silent thought
Sometimes I delve and find strange fancies there,
With heavy labour to the surface brought
That lie and mock me in the brighter air,
Poor ores from starvèd lodes of poverty,
Unfit for working or to be refined,
That in the darkness cheat the miner's eye,
I turn away from that base cave, the mind.
Yet had I but the power to crush the stone
There are strange metals hid in flakes therein,
Each flake a spark sole-hidden and alone,
That only cunning toilsome chemists win.
All this I know and yet my chemistry
Fails and the pregnant treasures useless lie.

8

X

The well-made sonnet takes the azure sea
Proud in her beauty as a halcyon,
Her timbers chosen words, and melody
Filling her sails of rhyme. She passes on
In majesty and calm, but these my lines
Are like a crazy and a leaky boat,
Clumsily made of warped and twisted pines
That hardly on the troubled waters float.
Now comes an arrogant great wave ahead
That swamps the blunted bow and spumes along ;
Into the storm I drift in doubt and dread,
Patient, not brave, enduring but not strong.
I know not on this huge and angry sea
How far my wretched ship can carry me.

MISCELLANEOUS POEMS

THE ONLY BEGETTER

THESE are not fair, except you walk with me,
  These heathery paths upon the wind-blown steep ;
There could no magic in the wild-flowers be,
  Save from your heart they drew it, wild and deep.

Round the vast world I turn and turn amazed
  Mine eyes grown keener for having looked on you
And what in the world has pleased me and I have praised
  Gives you through me again the praises due.

And have I other loves, what love have they
  Of mine, except what in your love I learnt,
In whose eyes first I saw immortal day,
  In whose arms first my sorrow to joy was burnt ?

Save as you taught, I could not see nor sing
  And all I sing is only in your praise,
And you the ultimate spirit of every thing
  That moves in my heart and colours my fleeting days.

SHADOWS

UNDER the leaves of that tremendous oak,
Where the low stars lie tangled, there is shade
Delusive and the leafy hedges fade
Into the darkness like a curling smoke.
        O in the shadow there,
Come with me, love, there let us two repair
To mingle with the darkness and be lost,
As somewhere viewless ghost with viewless ghost
May meet, caress and shiver with sweet pain,
Invisibly enamoured. So may we
Lie in each other's arms invisibly
And touch and see not, kiss and kiss again
        With lips obscure,
That find their way as ardent and as sure
        In darkness as in day.
Come! there the softly moving shadows play
And wrap all vision up for dim delight,
And soothe the straining eyes with oil of night,

14

That charms the senses, sends all sound to sleep
And knows for its anointed how to keep
A magic darkness, an enchanted hush,
Close in the shade of the uncertain bush.

Still the low stars shall waver overhead
And low clouds hang upon the mighty tree,
A softer darkness on our love to shed,
Where we embrace and kiss invisibly
    But tangibly,
And keener still, all senses being gone,
Save only one bright sense—save touch alone.

JUST THAT HALF-HOUR

Just that half-hour before you go to sleep,
Fold your tired hands together and repeat
All I have said to you of love to-day.
All that you can remember, I should say,
So many words and yet not all the same,
Still simple words and words that leapt like flame
Across the narrow gap between our hearts
And brutal words, strong, naked, stiff and stark,
Because our young love speaks in many ways.
. . . We are so young, we know not what to say
And yet the half-formed, ill-shaped words that fall
From untrained novice lips are musical
To untrained novice ears. If we are young
And say uncertainly what men have sung
In long dead years and still we do not know
All of love's arts, we'll be for ever so,
Untrained, unskilled, for this is far more sweet
Than love that treasures up and knows to keep
The secret arts of loving and being loved.

16

WASTE

So rich a treasure in yourself you bring,
That some is spilt and wasted on the way,
As low clouds, halting, on wild seas astray,
Cheat the thick, thirsty blossoms of the spring.
And some I waste. But in our later years
We shall remember how, too prodigal,
We let the precious drops of honey fall,
And pay for them at last with useless tears.
Ah, waste, waste, waste! However much there is,
There's not too much for bare and mortal days,
That now, receding in youth's golden haze,
Seem dim but ever full eternities.
But there's an end! Take heed, lest you and I
Have wasted wealth to think on when we die.

THE RETURN

Now into hearts long empty of the sun
The morning comes again with golden light
And all the shades of the half-dusk are done
And all the crevices are suddenly bright.
So gradually had love lain down to sleep,
We knew it not; but when we saw his head
Pillowed and sunken in a trance so deep
We whispered shuddering that he was dead.
Then you like Psyche took the light and leant
Over the monster lying in his place,
Daring, despairing, trembling as you bent . . .
But love raised up his new-awakening face
And into our hearts long empty of the sun
We felt the sky-distilled bright liquor run.

II

When love comes back that went in mist and cloud
He comes triumphant in his pomp and power;

Voices that muttered long are glad and loud
To mark the sweetness of the sudden hour.
How could we live so long in that half-light?
That opiate shadow, where the deadened nerves
So soon forget how hills and winds are bright,
That drugged and sleepy dusk, that only serves
With false shades to conceal the emptiness
Of hearts whence love has stolen unawares,
Where creeping doubts and dumb, dull sorrows press
And weariness with blind eyes gapes and stares.
This was our state, but now a happy song
Rings through our inner sunlight all day long.

III

When that I lay in a mute agony,
I nothing saw nor heard nor felt nor thought;
The inner self, the quintessential me,
In that blind hour beyond all sense was brought
Hard against pain. I had no body, no mind,
Nought but the point that suffers joy or loss,
No eyes in sudden blackness to be blind,
No brain for swift regrets to run across.
But when you touched me, when your hot tears fell,
The point that had been nothing else but pain

Changed into rapture by a miracle,
In which all raptures known before were vain.
Thus loss which bared the utmost shivering nerve
For joy's precursor in the heart did serve.

SONG

As I lay in the early sun,
Stretched in the grass, I thought upon
My true love, my dear love,
Who has my heart for ever,
Who is my happiness when we meet,
My sorrow when we sever.
She is all fire when I do burn,
Gentle when I moody turn,
Brave when I am sad and heavy
And all laughter when I am merry.
And so I lay and dreamed and dreamed,
And so the day wheeled on,
While all the birds with thoughts like mine
Were singing to the sun.

THE DEBT

WHEN I am dead and you gather up my poems,
    Put them all in, all those that speak of you,
Those that glanced at you in sundry disguises,
    Ariadne, Daphne and the nameless nymph,
The flower-bright queen who ruled a king in China,
    And the country-girl that early lost her love.
Bind up with them the frank and honest sonnets,
    The open songs, the unashamed odes,
That spoke straight to you and told that I loved you,
    Described your beauty or called you by name.
These are not ours ; for what I took of beauty
    Belongs to our fellows for whom I write.
The traces I have left on hill-top and valley
    Were made of the world and belong to the world ;
But more than half of the loveliness I captured
    Was yours at first and now is the world's.
Our first hidden kisses and unskilled embraces
    And the fierier love whereto we attained

Are lines on the chart whereby dreaming lovers
  Shall steer their hearts till the end of the world.
When we are dead and our ashes are scattered,
  Let them say of us : She was and he wrote.

THE FIELDS ARE FULL

The fields are full of summer still
   And breathe again upon the air
From brown dry side of hedge and hill
   More sweetness than the sense can bear.

So some old couple, who in youth
   With love were filled and over-full,
And loved with strength and loved with truth,
   In heavy age are beautiful.

FOR REMEMBRANCE

LET us remember how we came
  To Fletching in the trees,
Where stood the high and misty down
  Between us and the seas.

Let us remember how we crossed
  Ouse, Adur, Arun, three
Slight rivers rolling in their broad
  Green valleys to the sea.

Let us remember most of all
  When this bright air no more
We breathe, what young and morning oaths
  On the high hills we swore.

CONTINUITY

Long after we have ceased to be
The sun will light in bush and tree
And shine unchanged; the high turf hill
Shall stand up in beauty still;
And all the valleys that we knew
Put on again the summer's hue,
When we are gone, when we are gone,
And are what green things feed upon.

THE STORM

WE wake to hear the storm come down,
  Sudden on roof and pane ;
The thunder's loud and the hasty wind
  Hurries the beating rain.

The rain slackens, the wind blows gently,
  The gust grows gentle and stills,
And the thunder, like a breaking stick,
  Stumbles about the hills.

The drops still hang on leaf and thorn,
  The downs stand up more green ;
The sun comes out again in power
  And the sky is washed and clean.

A NIGHT-PIECE

To Arthur Geddes

COME out and walk. The last few drops of light
Drain silently out of the cloudy blue ;
The trees are full of the dark-stooping night,
    The fields are wet with dew.

All's quiet in the wood but, far away,
Down the hillside and out across the plain,
Moves, with long trail of white that marks its way,
    The softly panting train.

Come through the clearing. Hardly now we see
The flowers, save dark or light against the grass,
Or glimmering silver on a scented tree
    That trembles as we pass.

Hark now ! So far, so far . . . that distant song . . .
Move not the rustling grasses with your feet.
The dusk is full of sounds, that all along
    The muttering boughs repeat.

28

So far, so faint, we lift our heads in doubt.
Wind, or the blood that beats within our ears,
Has feigned a dubious and delusive note,
    Such as a dreamer hears.

Again . . . again ! The faint sounds rise and fail.
So far the enchanted tree, the song so low . . .
A drowsy thrush ? A waking nightingale ?
    Silence. We do not know.

THE FLOWERING TREES

THE wandering year from day to day discloses
First lenten lilies, then midsummer roses,
And ends at last in sombre fantasy,
About the season of the stripping tree,
With asters and dark daisies and the strange
Chrysanthemums. And so from change to change
The shimmering months proceed in shifting dresses
And strew the meadows and the wildernesses,
For there in grass the daffodils are born
And the wild rose-buds hanging on the thorn.
All these are good, but this perplexes me,
That blossom holds not longer on the tree,
For in the morning the tall pear stands white
With fragile petals that are shed at night,
And the apple wears her trembling sweet array
For hardly longer than a short spring day.
Would they might further live or would that I
Might see three springs without a break go by !

CLOUDS

Over this hill the high clouds float all day
And trail their long, soft shadows on the grass,
And now above the meadows make delay
And now with regular, swift motion pass.
Now comes a threatening drift from the south-west,
In smoky colours drest,
That spills far out upon the chequered plain
Its burden of dark rain ;
Then hard behind a stately galleon
Sails onward with its piled and carven towers
Stiff sculptured like a heap of marble flowers,
Rigid, unaltering, a miracle
Of moulded surfaces, whereon the light
Shines steadily, intolerably bright ;
Now on a livelier wind a wandering bell
Of delicate vapour comes, invisibly hung,
Like feathers from the seeding thistle flung,
And saunters wantonly far out of sight.

O God, who fill'st with shifting imagery
The blue page of the sky,
Thus writ'st thou also, with as vague a pen,
In the immenser hearts of dreaming men.

COLD

THE hard snow lies upon the hard round hills ;
Unbroken silence fills,
The empty valleys, and the unmoving air
Is thickened by the cold. The northward plain
Under a haze lies bleak and brown and bare,
Untouched by snow, and at its westerly rim
Loom dark and dim
The Malverns on the mist like a huge stain.

Turn, turn again
From that wet country to the snowy hills,
Where coldly in its silence the frost fills
The deep and rounded valleys with a fine
Jewel of air made crystalline.
The cold has frozen the air, the air's a gem,
Bright as a diamond filled with frozen light,
From the hill-tops down to the plain's wet hem,
Hard, yet clear to the sight.

Move not—we cannot move, we are prisoners,
Like that old traveller whom a later found
Within a shining ice-block straitly bound,
Staring immovably two hundred years
Across the waste, white ground.

ON HOLMBURY HILL

THE narrow paths branch every way up here
And cross and tangle and are nowhere clear
And the empty sky, swept clean by a rainy breath,
Smiles on our tortuous scrambling underneath.
But here's the top, for round a sudden bend
We stumble breathless on the unlooked for end
And stare across the misty weald. Below
The lonely trains through the wide country go,
Each with its plume of steam. And westward, see,
Past the far shoulder streams tumultuously
A black and driven storm across the air
And casts about the downs its troubled hair.
Thick at the middle, at the edges thinned,
Heeling over like a ship before the wind,
It eats the weald up with a greedy mouth.
Still, twenty miles or further to the south,
Dimly and grandly Chanctonbury stands
A moment clear above the blotted lands.
It's gone. But still the blue and empty sky
Smiles on over our heads unwittingly.

THE WISH

WOULD that I were away now
  From the iron streets and the steel sky,
For filthy are these streets in rain
  And hard and dusty dry.
Harshly the 'buses clang their way,
  The people are ugly that go by;
They hurry and their mouths are hard
  And they are hard of heart and eye.

I stand on the station every day
  To catch the crowded, swaying train
But if I only look down the line
  I turn away in sudden pain,
For an elm stands at the curve of the rail
  That beckons me out, out again,
Whether its leaves flash in the sun
  Or the bare boughs drip with rain.

The frost has my small town now
  And the street is iron there too,

For it stands in a high cup of the hills,
  Right in the north wind's view;
But the steel sky is beautiful there
  And the people that hurry there are few
And the bare hedges that catch the sun
  Tremble with frosty dew.

Though it be cold, I wish I were there
  To see slow winter move
And the elms growing green again
  And the blackthorn that I love.
Though spring's late there, it comes at last
  In the meadow and the thin beech-grove,
And happy I might lie there in May
  With a long green bough above.

MID-WINTER

WINTER hems us round ;
A powder of dry snow lies lightly on the ground ;
The cold stings our flesh and our hearts, perhaps, as well ;
Every faintest sound
Jars the quiet air like a harshly shaken bell.

The turning of the year
Was done a week ago, yet no light doth appear
And still the long nights eat the comfort-giving day.
Warmth draws not near ;
Not long enough to hearten us the sun doth stay.

Gentle, gentle sun,
Be our friend as of old for one day, only one.
Breathe deceitful life into us and everything,
Before happiness is done,
The happiness we need for the long months till spring.

THE GLOW-WORM

To Sylvia and Robert Lynd

THE pale road winds faintly upward into the dark skies,
And beside it on the rough grass that the wind invisibly stirs,
Sheltered by sharp-speared gorse and the berried junipers,
Shining steadily with a green light, the glow-worm lies.

We regard it ; and this hill and all the other hills
That fall in folds to the river, very smooth and steep,
And the hangers and brakes that the darkness thickly fills
Fade like phantoms round the light and night is deep, so
    deep,—

That all the world is emptiness about the still flame
And we are small shadows standing lost in the huge night.
We gather up the glow-worm, stooping with dazzled sight,
And carry it to the little enclosed garden whence we came,

And place it on the short grass. Then the shadowy flowers
    fade,
The walls waver and melt and the houses disappear
And the solid town trembles into insubstantial shade
Round the light of the burning glow-worm, steady and clear.

THE CATACLYSM

When a great wave disturbs the ocean cold
   And throws the bottom waters to the sky,
   Strange apparitions on the surface lie,
Great battered ships, stripped of their gloss and gold,
And, writhing in their pain, sea-monsters old,
   Who stain the waters with a bloody dye,
   With unaccustomed mouths bellow and cry
And vex the waves with struggling fin and fold.

And with these too come little trivial things
   Tossed from the deeps by the same casual hand ;
   A faint sea flower, dragged from the lowest sand,
That will not undulate its luminous wings
In the slow tides again, lies dead and swings
   Along the muddy ripples to the land.

IN ABSENCE

My lovely one, be near to me to-night
For now I need you most, since I have gone
Through the sparse woodland in the fading light,
Where in time past we two have walked alone,
Heard the loud nightjar spin his pleasant note
And seen the wild rose folded up for sleep
And whispered, though the soft word choked my throat,
Your dear name out across the valley deep.
Be near to me, for now I need you most.
To-night I saw an unsubstantial flame
Flickering along those shadowy paths, a ghost
That turned to me and answered to your name,
Mocking me with a wraith of far delight.
. . . My lovely one, be near to me to-night.

THE RIDDLE

I DREAM the marriage of the visible
With the unseen. the solving of all skeins ;
I dream that in my verse I read the spell,
The last answer to the world's delights and pains,
The gleaming leaves of beeches, the shade thrown
By wavering ripples on the stream-worn stone,
The glowing green of the young wheat, the cries
    Of birds, the lapsing sighs
Of spring's warm airs in lucent hedge and tree,
All these and with these too the discontent
Of life's frustration and the vanity
Of happiness too casually spent—
    All these I contemplate
And would the seeming with the real fuse,
The lordly vesture with the spirit mate,
And publish in great verse the immortal news.

Still the dream fades ; and closer home doth dwell,
Living with me, whether I sleep or wake,
What neither here nor there my hand can take ;
Hidden in love lies the unriddled spell,
Nearest the heart and there least scrutable.

THE SINGER

In the dim light of the golden lamp
  The singer stands and sings,
And the songs rise up like coloured bubbles
  Or birds with shining wings.

And the movement of the merry or plaintive keys
  Sounds in the silent air
Till the listener feels the room no more
  But only music there.

And still from the sweet and rounded mouth
  The delicate songs arise,
Like floating bubbles whose colours are
  The coloured melodies.

LADY GODIVA

(A third version.)

If the truth were but known, when she came at last
To the bower's low door and the journey was past,
Godiva slid from her palfrey and said :
Only one with a curious eye in his head ?

For why had she gone with not even a shift
Through the still grey streets, where her hair's gold drift
On shoulder and breast and side made one
With the bright veil cast on her by the sun ?

O surely it had been braver, and sweet,
To have lavished her beauty along the street,
To have ridden in the eyes and the smiles of the crowd
And to have heard their praises, muttered or loud.

For else her ride was only a ride,
Nothing done, nothing given, nothing beside,
No shame, no sacrifice made, no pain,
But a fresh, cool journey and home again.

She frowned as she stood up bare in her bower,
White as a pearl and fresh as a flower,
Then smiled as she thought that there had been one
And that Peeping Tom was better than none.

SEARCHLIGHTS

(In the manner of Paul Fort.)

O SEARCHLIGHTS, pierce the night with swords and drive
the stars in ruin thence; the moon in cold indifference
looks down upon your leaping hordes.

Storm the old ramparts of the sky and shake the planets
all awry, pull, if you can, the young moon down upon the
house-tops of the town.

The rosy sky adrowsing lay but now the night's alive
with fire, new pulses in the veins of night, quick phantoms
of a fiercer fire.

Then fly, bright clouds, across the air and meet and
interchange and merge and flood the sky with flame, sub-
merge the planets in your ghostly glare.

O not with swords you now invade the ancient kingdom
of the stars but armed with soft and fluent blades you break
black heaven's tremendous bars

and seize those pale and stately lights that move and move invisibly and whirl them up and down the sky, your followers, your satellites !

And while across the night you fling your blue and brilliant garlanding, even the cold, indifferent moon moves gaily to a soundless tune ;

and all the shades that used to lie still in the silent streets and sleep, rise up and move fantastically in time with you and leap and leap !

INVITATION

O GIRL with honey-coloured hair,
  And will you come and dance with me?
The night is dark but you can spare
  Light from your eyes for both to see,
And in the shade of trees divine
Like a whirled torch your hair will shine.

So dance apart and dance away;
  The rest about the lanterns gather,
But there is light for two to play
  In any place where we're together,
And there is soft long grass and shadow
Beneath the rick across the meadow.

For love in darkness is at ease
  And likes no candle save the light
Of kindled eyes and glowing tress
  And bodies luminous with delight.
The rest about the candles stay:
O dance away! O come away!

BALLAD

HE

Oh, where are you, my own true love,
  And why are you not here?
The nightingale amid the boughs
  Is flattering his dear.

The night among the empty fields
  Lies like a child at rest,
But empty, empty are my arms
  And light, too light my breast.

SHE

If you had known what I have known,
  The harsh word and the blow,
The sour meal and the heavy task,
  You would not chide me so.

O, I go on through all the day,
  And only hope at night,

That I may slip out silently
  Without a sup or bite,

That I may find you in the dark,
  Wherein you will not see
The angry red that rims my eyes
  And burns them bitterly.

You have not felt what I have felt;
  This only have you known
That it is sweet to walk with me
  In the dark fields alone.

You only hear me speak of love
  And you have never heard
My father's thin and grumbling voice,
  My mother's heavy word.

Yet, ah, the most I know of you
  Is nothing more than this
That when the painful day is done
  Your lips are good to kiss.

THE KING'S DANCER

It was the king of the East, they say, who bought
A slave-girl in the market of Baghdad.
The merchants brought her thither, travelling
A long way southward, from the wrinkled hills
Of Georgia and sold her for a price.
It was the king who saw her, as he passed
At midday through the hot and narrow streets,
And asked what sum they set on her. They told him.
He bade his purse-bearer count out the coins
And bring her home. But when he saw her first
Among the fountains and the misty leaves
In the cool garden of his golden house,
He loved her.

          She would dance for his delight
And when she entertained him thus, he stared,
Stupid with pleasure. She was young and nimble,
With subtly moving wrists of ivory
And ankles finer and stronger than graven steel.
She was the blossoming bough that stirs in spring,

The pearl-white clouds that drift across blue heaven,
The rainbowed wave that dies in colour on
A sunny shore, the wheeling flight of birds
Hardly descried against a dusky wood,
The arrowy darting fish in quiet brooks ;
All the earth's myriad movements lay in her.
The king sat in his jewelled seat and saw
With deep, fixed eyes her motions flash and blend
In convolutions of the astounding dance,
And ever when she paused he signed her on,
Silently staring.
                    She danced all through the night,
Now in slow measure mimed the rising moon,
And now in a frenzy of light and hurrying steps
The scattered and stricken clouds that fly in shreds
Across the face of the moon and are lost in night
And die in bitter space for love of the moon.
Still with his grave deep eyes the king applauded,
Silently nodding, and when she paused for rest,
He raised his great arm up and with hairy fingers
Urged her to dancing. Dark lines beneath her eyes
And sharp lines at the corners of her mouth
Grew as night grew and weariness invaded
Even her limbs of pearl and steel. She wept
Small and infrequent tears of pain, hard wrung
From a brave heart and body. Still she danced

And when dawn shot his blood-red flames across
The shimmering fountains and drowned the garden in gold,
She sank in a last, triumphant attitude,
Her bosom open to the rising sun.

So the king loved her and he built for her
A bright pavilion hidden in high trees
And there at night he came to visit her,
Without his retinue. Two, Nubian soldiers
Alone attended him to ward away
The attempts of the wicked and remained on guard
While he was in. So when his pleasure bade,
He came to her and watched her maddening dance
Or took her on his knees and fondled her
And praised her lovely body of pearl and steel
With silent glances and silent straying hands,
Her body that was, so often as she danced,
A flickering flame, an insubstantial wreath
Of linkèd movements.
                        But he came one night
Through the black shadows of the mighty trees,
Black and immense beneath the risen moon,
Unseen, unheard. The negroes crept behind,
Blotted in shade. He picked his way to the gate
And through the filigree of coilèd gold
He saw her little garden full of light,

Wherein she danced alone and not for him,
But with her moonwhite arms to the risen moon
She offered her beauty and her sacred steps.
An hour he stood unmoving; an hour she moved
In measures of unbelievable loveliness,
A phantasy of night; the essential wraith
Of the moon, as though the light that filled the place
Were thicker at the centre and there took
A bodily shape and grew to be a woman,
That danced and danced for silence and the moon.

But when the light was gone, he turned away
And sought his negroes in the deeper shadow.
They came to him, darkness in darkness disguised;
He drew them close and spoke in a low still voice,
And, pointing with his hand to the pavilion,
Commanded: Let the woman's ankles be broken.

POSTSCRIPT TO A SATIRE ON MODERN ENGLISH POETRY

Brooke's dead and Flecker; almost with them died
Our new-born poetry in all her pride
And one in Scyros sleeps and one at home,
Brothers dissevered by the careless foam.
Their youth bore blossoms; but an unnatural frost
Gave to them youth for ever at the cost
That neither should bear fruit nor ripen on
To fertile age beneath a kindlier sun.
Two yet we have; Hodgson and De la Mare
In that dark year relenting death did spare,
Sick of his work. Our poetry survives
And bears new fruit in those most happy lives.
Them let us cherish; and, loving them, let us learn
To leave our railing and with new songs to burn.

FÊTE GALANTE; THE TRIUMPH OF LOVE

Aristonoë, the fading shepherdess,
Gathers the young girls round her in a ring,
Teaching them wisdom of love,
What to say, how to dress,
How frown, how smile,
How suitors to their dancing feet to bring,
How in mere walking to beguile,
What words cunningly said in what a way
Will draw man's busy fancy astray,
All the alphabet, grammar and syntax of love.

The garden smells are sweet,
Daisies spring in the turf under the high-heeled feet,
Dense, dark banks of laurel grow
Behind the wavering row
Of golden, flaxen, black, brown, auburn heads,
Behind the light and shimmering dresses

Of these unreal, modern shepherdesses ;
And gaudy flowers in formal patterned beds
Vary the dim long vistas of the park,
Far as the eye can see,
Till at the forest's edge the ground grows dark
And the flowers vanish in the obscurity.

The young girls gather round her,
Remembering eagerly how their fathers found her
Fresh as a spring-like wind in February,
Subtler in her moving heart than sun-motes that vary
At every waft of an opening and shutting door ;
They gather chattering near,
Hush, break out in laughter, whisper aside,
Grow silent more and more,
Though she will never chide.
Now through the silence sounds her voice still clear,
And all give ear.

Like a silver thread through the golden afternoon,
Equably the voice discloses
All that age-old wisdom ; like an endless tune
Aristonoë's voice wavers among the roses,
Level and unimpassioned,
Telling them how of nothing love is fashioned,
How it is but a movement of the mind,

Bidding Celia mark
That light skirts fluttering in the wind
Or white flowers stuck in dark,
Glistening hair have fired the dull beholder
Or telling Anais
That faint indifference ere now hath bred a kiss
Denied to flaunted snowy breast or shoulder.

The girls attend,
Each thinking on her friend,
Whether he be real or imaginary,
Whether he be loving or cold,
For each ere she grows old
Means to pursue her joy and the whole unwary
Troop of their wishes has this wild quarry in cry,
That draws them ineluctably,
More and more as the summer slippeth by.
And Celia leans aside
To contemplate her black-silked ankle on the grass ;
In remote dreaming pride,
Rosalind recalls the image in her glass.
Phillis through all her body feels
How divine energy steals,
Quiescent power and resting speed,
Stretches her arms out, feels the warm blood run

Ready for pursuit, for strife and deed,
And turns her glowing face up to the sun.
Phillida smiles
And lazily trusts her lazy wit,
A slow arrow that hath often hit ;
Chloe, bemused by many subtle wiles,
Grows not more dangerous for all of it.
But opens her red lips, yawning drowsily,
And shows her small white teeth,
Dimpling the round chin beneath,
And stretches, moving her young body deliciously.

And still the lesson goes on,
For this is an old story that is never done
And now the precept is of ribbon and shoe,
What with linens and silks love finds to do
And how man's heart is tangled in a string
Or taken in gauze like a weak and helpless thing.
Chloe falls asleep ; and the long summer day
Drifts slowly past the girls and the warm roses,
Giving in dreams its hours away.
Now Stella throws her head back and Phillis disposes
Her strong brown hands quietly in her lap
And Rose's slender feet grow restless and tap
The turf to an imaginary tune.
Now all this grace of youthful bodies and faces

Is wrought to a glow by the golden weather of June ;
Now, Love, completing grace of all the graces,
Strong in these hearts thy pure streams rise,
Transmuting what they learn by heavenly alchemies.
Swift from the listeners the spell vanishes,
And through the tinkling, empty words,
True thoughts of true love press,
Flying and wheeling nearer,
As through a sunny sky a flock of birds
Against the throbbing blue grows clearer and clearer,
So closer come these thoughts and dearer.

Helen rises with a laugh ;
Chloe wakes ;
All the enchantment scatters off like chaff,
The cord is loosened and the spell breaks.
Rosalind
Resolves that to-night she will be kind to her lover,
Unreflecting, warm and kind.
Celia tells the lessons over,
Counting on her fingers—one and two. . . .
Ribbon and shoe,
Skirts, flowers, song, dancing, laughter, eyes. , . .
Through the whole catalogue of formal gallantry
And studious coquetries,
Counting to herself maliciously.

But the old, the fading shepherdess, Aristonoë,
Rises stiffly and walks alone
Down the broad path where densely the laurels grow,
And over a little lawn, not closely mown,
Where wave the flowering grass and the rich meadow-sweet.
She seems to walk painfully now and slow
And drags a little on her high-heeled feet.
She stops at last below
An old and twisted plum-tree, whose last petal is gone,
Leans on the comfortable, rugged bole
And stares through the green leaves at the drooping sun.
The tree and the warm light comfort her aging soul.

On the other lawn behind her, out of sight,
The girls at play
Drive out melancholy by lively delight
And the wind carries their songs and laughter away.
Some begin dancing and seriously tread
A modern measure up and down the grass,
Turn, slide with bending knees and pass
With dipping hand and poising head,
Float through the sun in pairs, like newly shed
And golden leaves astray
Upon the warm wind of an autumn day,
When the Indian summer rules the air.

Others, having found,
Lying idly on the sun-hot ground,
Shuttlecocks and battledores,
Play with the buoyant feathers and stare
Dazzled at the plaything as it soars,
Vague against the shining sky,
Where light yet throbs and confuses the eye,
Then see it again, white and clear,
As slowly, poisèdly it falls by
The dark green foliage and floats near.
But Celia, apart, is pensive and must sigh
And Anais but faintly pursues the game.
An encroaching, inner flame
Burns in their hearts with the acrid smoke of unrest ;
But gaiety runs like quicksilver in Rose's breast
And Phillis, rising,
Walks by herself with high and springy tread,
All her young blood racing from heels to head,
Breeding new desires and a new surprising
Strength and determination,
Whereof are bred
Confidence and joy and exultation.

The long day closes ;
Rosalind's hour draws near, and Chloe's and Rose's,

The hour that Celia has prayed,
The hour for which Anais and Stella have stayed,
When Helen shall forget her wit
And Phillida by a sure arrow at length be hit.
And Phillis, the fleet runner, be at length overtaken,
When this bough of young blossoms
By the rough, eager gatherers shall be shaken.
Their eyes grow dim,
Their hearts flutter like taken birds in their bosoms,
As the light dies out of heaven,
And a faint, delicious tremor runs through every limb,
And faster the volatile blood through their veins is driven.

The long day closes ;
The last light fades in the amber sky ;
Warm through the warm dusk glow the roses
And a heavier shade drops slowly from the trees,
While through the garden as all colours die
The scents come livelier on the quickening breeze.
The world grows larger, vaguer, dimmer,
Over the dark laurels, a few faint stars glimmer ;
The moon, that was a pallid ghost,
Hung low on the horizon, faint and lost,
Comes up, a full and splendid golden round
By black and sharp-cut foliage overcrossed.
The girls laugh and whisper now with hardly a sound

Till all sound vanishes, dispersed in the night,
Like a wisp of cloud that fades in the moon's light
And the garden grows silent and the shadows grow
Deeper and blacker below
The mysteriously moving and murmuring trees,
That stand out darkly against the star-luminous sky ;
Huge stand the trees,
Shadowy, whispering immensities,
That rain down quietude and darkness on heart and eye.
None move, none speak, none sigh,
But from the laurels comes a leaping voice
Crying in tones that seem not man's or boy's
But only joy's,
And hard behind a loud tumultuous crying,
A tangled skein of noise,
And the girls see their lovers come, each vieing
Against the next in glad and confident poise
Or softly moving
To the side of the chosen with gentle words and loving
Gifts for her pleasure of sweetmeats and jewelled toys.

Dear Love, whose strength no pedantry can stir,
Whether in thine iron enemies
Or in thine own strayed follower,
Bemused with subtleties and sophistries,

Now dost thou rule the garden, now
The gatherers' hands have grasped the scented bough.

Slow the sweet hours resolve and one by one are sped.
The garden lieth empty. Overhead
A nightjar rustles by, wing touching wing,
And passes, uttering
His hoarse and whirring note.
The daylight birds long since are fled,
Nor has the moon yet touched the brown bird's throat.
All's quiet, all is silent, all around
The day's heat rises gently from the ground
And still the broad moon travels up the sky,
Now glancing through the trees and now so high
That all the garden through her rays are shed
And from the laurels one can just descry
Where in the distance looms enormously
The old house, with all its windows black and dead.

WHO KNOWS HOW BEAUTY SPRINGS

WHO knows how beauty springs
Out of the world of things,
To take the eyes with sudden flame
And vanish whence it came,
High above things that vex,
Fear, covetousness, spite and sex?

Lost in the busy day,
In thoughts that harry and press,
I knew a young girl passed
And heard her swinging dress;
And when I turned I saw,
Raised on a stair,
Only her ankle, finely poised
Against the coloured air.

Who that has known can tell
How in this world of things,
Suddenly in the dark day,
Eternal beauty springs?

THE WILD GOOSE CHASE

How long a day through thickets and over stones
   And over broad red furrows fresh from the plough,
And hills where low the wind-bent heather drones
   And swift airs whistle round the sky-line bough !
How the wind clutched at flesh and bowels and bones !
   How breathless they were all day, how weary now,
When in the town beneath a fading light
They sought a lodging for their transient night.

What in what frenzy did they thus pursue ?
   Eternal wisdom or the baser gold
Or pleasures of the senses ever new
   Or rarer spiritual ecstasies still untold ?
From dawn till dusk, with sun, wind, hills, rain, dew,
   They were burnt or they were weary or they were cold
Or wet or dirty. Still they chased untired
A thing not named but endlessly desired.

68

But when the chase was done at last, they came
  Into the darkling town with empty hands;
Their faces through the dusk burnt with a flame
  Wind caught, their feet were heavy from marshy lands.
They brought with them no answer to their proud claim,
  No prize given over to their loud demands;
They found an inn, where windows long and low
Streaked the thick darkness with a golden glow.

Inns of our nights, where we have sat together,
  Boots off and dreaming at the magic fire!
There the mind's free, the spirit casts its tether
  The thoughts in concert dance and do not tire,
Till sleep with silent foot and sudden feather
  Brushes his drugs across the joy and desire
And all long night is darkness and deep peace,
In the old inn, walled round with silent trees.

The happy good find this when the day is spent,
  When they have filled their day with seeing and knowing.
Here from their chase they came and found content
  And reaped at night good grain of early sowing,
Laughter by tears and joy by sorrow lent
  And gifts on unexpected breezes blowing—
We too shall sit, after youth's fret and rage,
In the comfortable bar of middle age.

Yet while light burns and the air aches in our veins
    And we are capable of anger and love,
Slow fires of the senses, swift play of the brains
    And tenderness and friendliness enough,
We will be out in the winds, the dews, the rains,
    And find our meaning in such transient stuff,
While through sharp, veering gusts of tears and mirth,
We chase our wild geese over the windy earth.

HYMN TO DESIRE

To Linda Chesterman

Not only when thou art terrible, Desire,
  Do we acknowledge thine unshaken power ;
Thou liv'st not only in the raging fire,
  Thou liv'st as fully in the slightest flower.
Now the moon fails, that radiant so long
  Rode the black, burnished levels of the night,
  Serene and lovely witness of delight ;
And now I catch my breath and hold my song,
  That cannot longer than the heaven be bright,
For the faint clouds that now obscure the moon
Darken my mind's serenity too soon.

Thus is it ever. Still the shade will creep
  On lovely things, who knoweth how or whence ?
Like quick dreams crowding in a healthy sleep,
  A sudden pulse, an urgent influence.
Thus the light wrinkles on an azure pool

71

Spread outward from the fall of one frail leaf,
  The first the tree weeps off for future grief,
In the sad hour when summer's cup is full.
  Long move the waters, though the touch be brief,
And break in shards that image of the sky
They showed before in blue tranquillity.

Who knoweth how or whence desire will come,
  The wind that wakes the foam-line on the sea,
That breathes new feeling into spirits numb
  To try again an exquisite agony?
Maybe when in the idle world of men,
  We poise in words upon the perfect hour
  Or, lonely, stoop to touch a lonely flower,
At the serenest point of noon or when
  A black cloud breaks into a silver shower;
Out of all these and out of more than these
The influence comes that shatters all our ease.

I too have prayed to feel desire no more,
  To find in little things a small content,
No longer from the green and friendly shore
  To swim, a waif in the huge element.
My spirit darkens, my heart beats fitfully;
  A power descends upon my soul that shakes
  The calm of tranquillising song and breaks

The doom-dark wave of passion over me
  And every tumult in my being wakes;
A power not friendly to me but divine
Troubles the current of my trembling line.

In all the things we love the ambush lies
  And most of all in love. Who has not known'
Under the glance of the belovèd's eyes
  How painfully his deep unrest has grown ?
Out of sweet things we would a refuge make,
  A certain harbour for the flying mind,
  Each worldly solace to our fortune bind,
Comfort from love, counsel from friendship take ;
  Yet in the roof and furnishings we find,
Hid like a snake, whose fangs bear venomous fire,
Thou hast thy secret shelter made, Desire !

O most of all in love ! Contentment there
  Is but the single moment ere decay,
Precursor of a long and dull despair,
  Frets the fruit's golden rind and flesh away.
Some wear love's crown a day and see love go,
  Having been content ; but they whose loves endure
  Ache with an ill love has not strength to cure,
Strive for perfection, stumble still and know
  Too well that love is ever insecure,

That in the midst of pleasure hunger sits
And feeds upon the tortured heart and wits.

Immortal agony ! what canst thou be,
  If that thou be not the immortal spur,
Which, when we halt in sloth or luxury,
  We faint and failing mortals must incur ?
Thus comes the wind upon a mountain-lake
    That lay beneath the sun, serene and bland ;
    And now at touch of the triumphant hand
A thousand colours on the surface wake ;
    The ripples move and curl from land to land
And, while they struggle and the tyrant blows,
The tumult of the sunlit water grows.

The faint clouds drift and drive across the moon,
    Veil and unveil her distant loveliness ;
The ecstasy will sink and leave me soon,
    Yet still the vague, bright intimations press
Remorselessly upon my flagging mind,
    And to these whips my shuddering flesh lies bare
    And to these lights my aching eyeballs stare—
I wince, my courage leaves me, I am blind !
    O spare me utter death but mostly spare
The dull revengeful fire, the mocking prize
Which in the heart of all fulfilment lies,

For all fulfilment let lament be made,
    Save for the pause and turning which is death ;
Weep for those spirits who on shows that fade
    And earthly copies waste their fitful breath,
Forgetful of the far, ideal skies.
    They know not how the awakened soul can be
    Borne above sorrow and felicity
To hold brief converse thus with Paradise
    And catch the signals of eternity ;
They know not that desire is but a spray
Thrown from the fountain of eternal day !

The moon is gone, the moon is down and dead ;
    A last dull gleam in the horizon trees
Bears witness to the glory that is shed ;
    Now through the vacant sky a rambling breeze
Murmurs invisibly. The wings now fail
    That bore aloft my struggling load of song.
    I faint, I falter. Be thou now not long,
O sleep unwaked of owl or nightingale,
    Nor let not in on me the urgent throng
Of dreams, but be thou full and calm and deep,
For more than this I crave not, blessèd sleep !

A DIALOGUE

Long have I striven and now am overwrought
With sleepless nights and days whose blackened suns
Make pale my blood and drain my spirit of fire,
Mine eyes of light.

                —But spring will come again.
—But not again that old ideal spring,
The essence of the Aprils that have been
And live as memories. All that is lost ;
Now, even in my six and twentieth year,
Like winter twilight in a little room,
Over the wide expanse of wood and field,
Slow darkness thickens in the room of the world,
Which with the lamps of science and poetry
I must illuminate as best I can.
—But there is life beyond this darkening life.
Somewhere behind the narrow arch of blue
Dwell the imaginable verities
Which you have seen and whose remembered forces
Draw your sick heart in longing from your breast.

—They are there indeed but I am cast on earth.
After how long and how headlong a fall
I here reside ! where there is nothing true
But shadows and faint copies that suggest
Dimly and brokenly the real world,
Whence we are exiled here. O, how can I
See the truth shine beyond phantasmal shows
And thin the splendour of the gorgeous earth
And still be glad for either ?
                                        —But your spirit
Remembers yet the home from which you came
And gives ideal beauty to the fragments
And wreckage of this unpieced, fantastic life.
—Would it were so ! The world in which we live
Was once my pleasure. Midday gleaming elms
And silent oaks with brooding night in their boughs
And the low-chanting aspens and the holy
Unreal thorn ablaze with silver flowers,
Whether amid the odorous meadows set
Or on the sides of smooth and lofty hills,
Delighted me and then were nought but trees.
The rayless blue of heavy August skies
Pleased me, and the clouds that floated stiffly past
Were solid toys that vision touched and played with.
I found my joy in beautiful forms and in
The fresh and supple body of my young love,

Her voice, her eyes, her arms about my neck,
And in all girls that passed me in the streets,
Light with the grace of youth and happy pride,
In colours and music and the lovely words
That then could bind my sorrows up with spells,
Such sorrows as then I knew. But now through these
Shines the intolerable sum of truth,
Gleams through the misty veil
Of the world's beauty and makes poor and thin
This life's imperfect grace.
                              —Yet do you not
Strive for perfection still,
Strain and glow warm in straining for the truth?
Are not the joys you had from earthly things
Transformed by musing on the original?
—Would it were so!
                              —Yet have you no inner faith
That from the mist of illusion you will at length
Emerge and move about the real world?
—Thence have I fallen far and farther fall
Headlong in ruin through these empty cheats.
Why should I hope (since hope is also a cheat)
Ever to find again that tangled way
I followed hither from eternity?
Still through the waste of dark and whirling time,

Through shadowed years and sombre centuries,
My spirit goes, like a lost child in a wood,
Crying for home amid the unfriendly boughs
And straying further from the invisible road.

MEDITATION IN JUNE, 1917

I

How can we reason still, how look afar,
  Who, these three years now, are
Drifting, poor flotsam hugely heaved and hurled
  In the birthday of a world,
Upon the waves of the creative sea?
  How gain lucidity
Or even keep the faith wherewith at first
  We met the storm that burst,
The singing hope of revolution's prime?
  For in that noble time
We saw the petty world dissolve away
  And fade into a day
Where dwelt new spirits of a better growth,
  Unchecked by spite and sloth.
We saw, and even now we seem to see
  In fitful revery,
Like hills obscured and hid by earthly mist,
  The hopes that first we kissed:

We see them—catch at them and lose again
  In apathy and pain
What maybe was (though it once seemed ours to hold)
  No more than fairy gold.

II

We pity those whom quick death overtakes,
  Though they will never see
How hope dissolves and founded loyalty shakes
  Traitorously, piteously.
They lose at most and death is voiceless still
  Nor whispers in their ears
When they are lying on the deep-scarred hill
  What our calm silence hears.
They lose all various life, they lose the day,
  The clouds, the winds, the rain,
The blossoms down an English road astray
  They will not see again;
Great is their loss but more tremendous things
  To us at home are given,
Doubts, fears and greeds and shameful waverings
  That hide the blood-red heaven.
They knew no doubt and fear was soon put by:
  Freely their souls could move
In deeds that gave new life to loyalty,
  A sharper edge to love.

They are the conquerors, the happy dead,
  Who gave their lives away,
And now amid the trenches where they bled,
  Forgetful of the day,
Deaf, blind and unaware, sleep on and on,
  Nor open eyes to weep,
Know nought of what is ended or begun
  But only and always sleep.

III

We said on that first day, we said and swore
  That self should be no more,
That we were risen, that we would wholly be
  For love and liberty;
And in the exhilaration of that oath
  We cast off spite and sloth
And laboured for an hour, till we began,
  Man after piteous man,
To lose the splendour, to forget the dream
  And leave our noble theme,
To find again our lusts and villainies
  And seek a baser prize;
This we have done and what is left undone
  Cries out beneath the sun.
How glad a dawn fades thus in foggy night,
  Where not a star shines bright!

IV

Is all then gone ?   That nobler morning mood
When pain appeared an honour and grief a gift
And what was difficult was also good ?
Are all our wishes on the waves adrift ?
The young, the eager-hearted, they are gone,
And we, the stay-at-homes, are tired and old,
Careless how carelessly our work is done,
Forgetful how that morning rose in gold
When all our hearts cried out in unison,
Triumphant in the new triumphal sun.
How dull a night succeeds ! how dark and cold !
We will arise.   Oh, not as then with singing,
But silence in our mouths and no word said,
Though wracks of that lost glory round us clinging
Shame us with broken oaths we swore the dead,
But steadfast in humility we rise,
Hoping no glory, having merited none,
Through the long night to toil with aching eyes
And pray that our humbler hearts may earn the sun.

ELEGY

(For J.N., died of wounds, October, 1916.)

So you are dead. We lived three months together,
   But in these years how absence can divide !
We did not meet again. I wonder whether
   You thought of me at all before you died.

There in that whirl of unaccustomed faces,
   Strange, friendless, ill, I found in you a friend—
And then at last in these divided places,
   For you in France and here for me the end.

For friendship's memory was short and faithless
   And time went by that will not come again,
And you are dead of wounds and I am scatheless
   Save as my heart has sorrowed for my slain.

I wonder whether you were long in dying,
   Where, in what trench and under what dim star,
With drawn face on the clayey bottom lying,
   While still the untiring guns cried out afar.

I might have been with you, I might have seen you
  Reel to the shot with blank and staring eye,
I might have held you up . . . I might have been you
  And lain instead of you where now you lie.

Here in our quietude strange fancy presses,
  Dark thoughts of woe upon the empty brain,
And fills the streets and the pleasant wildernesses
  With forms of death and ugly shapes of pain.

You are long dead. A year is nearly over,
  But still your voice leaps out again amid
The tangled memories that lie and cover
  With countless trails what then we said and did.

And still in waking dreams I sit and ponder
  Pleasures that were and, as my working brain
Deeper in revery will stray and wander,
  I think that I shall meet with you again

And make my plans and half arrange the meeting,
  And half think out the words that will be said
After the first brief, careless, pleasant greeting. . . .
  Then suddenly I remember you are dead.

THE HALT

" Mark time in front ! Rear fours cover ! Company—halt !
Order arms ! Stand at—ease ! Stand easy." A sudden hush :
And then the talk began with a mighty rush—
" You weren't ever in step—The sergeant.—It wasn't my
       fault—
Well, the Lord be praised at least for a ten minutes' halt."
  We sat on a gate and watched them easing and shifting ;
  Out of the distance a faint, keen breath came drifting,
From the sea behind the hills, and the hedges were salt.

Where do you halt now ? Under what hedge do you lie ?
  Where the tall poplars are fringing the white French roads?
And smoke I have not seen discolours the foreign sky ?
Is the company resting there as we rested together
  Stamping its feet and readjusting its loads
And looking with wary eyes at the drooping weather ?

THE FIRELESS TOWN.

THE FIRELESS TOWN

BENEATH a rising wood there was a town
That had in ancient times its own renown,
For in a valley rich and warm it lay
And there through interwoven boughs the day
Came softly stealing and burning brighter, till
The broad sun rose above the topmost hill.
A long way west, the broad and level plains,
White with the dew or filled with morning rains,
Stirred in the dawn and shook a myriad leaves
Over the flanks of silky-coated beeves,
And there great fields of green or yellow corn
With lifting heads the seasons did adorn,
While acres much more odorous lay between,
Bee-pleasing clover and the scented bean,
And orchards, where long loaded boughs hung down,
Parted the open country and the town.
It was a portly place, because therein
A many merchants mighty gain did win

By bartering the farmers' rich increase,
Or wool much wealthier than the Golden Fleece,
Wherewith they built great halls of yellow stone
And set tall windowed gables thereupon
And hoarded in their houses gold and gem
And silk and silver vessels. One of them
A daughter had, of whom the story is,
In beauty blest and maiden innocencies.
Her name was Helen and her heart was proud,
For though much loved she had not loved nor bowed
To be a toy for any man or hear
Love's subtle offers urged by any whisperer.
Yet in the flesh she was divinely made ;
Her honey-shining hair in heavy braid
Clung round her temples, as the sunset lies
On snowy mountain ridges and her eyes
Burnt like the heaven's warm and candid grey
When August spends in fire his dreamy day ;
Straight as an arrow, as a birch-tree tall,
Where maidens met she overcame them all.
So she was made ; but how she looked and moved
Could not be told by them that most her loved.
They watched her with the young girls, when she came
And danced with them, a light and errant flame,
Cool fire that flickered and was not consumed
But burnt more radiant as the dark trees gloomed

With drooping night. They worshipped her when she
Advanced her narrow ankles delicately
Or turned on flashing heels or quickly span
Around the ring with light skirts swaying as she ran.
When she was walking, it was strange how went
Her nimble pace upon the pavèment,
How easily she climbed the steepest hill
And laughed upon the crest, untroubled still;
She spoke as though a nightingale had rested
Within her rising bosom and there nested,
Contented with one climate all the year,
Where every morning still gay summer did appear.
In many suitors found she lovers none :
Of all that prayed to her she chose not one.
At nightfall by the lanthorn light she stayed
While her companions of the sun delayed
With other friends to saunter in the wood
So softly that the light awakened brood
Of crying birds that harboured there slept on
Nor knew what hid, delightful things were done,
What gifts refused and what at last were given
Beneath the friendly, close and leaf-embroidered heaven.
Some maidens came back silently and some
Loud in their joy along the dark streets home
And some came weeping ; but ere all were come

Helen slept dreamless in her narrow bed,
Her body lying straight, her quiet head
Still on the pillow and her quiet eyes
Peacefully rid of day's quick vanities.
Though all men praised, her father praised her more
Because he slept at night with unlocked door,
Unshuttered windows and a heart at rest,
While all his fellows at the inn confessed
That bars and bolts must keep their daughters in
And roving dishonour from the anxious kin.
Young men reviled what gave him quiet blood;
Pale were their sullen faces, who had stood
All night beneath her window, that all night
Denied the least reply of flattering light,
Grated no sound, however harsh or small,
But blindly stared and answered not at all.
They lingered in the dark and Helen lay
Unmoved in careless sleep until the day
Despatched them hollow-eyed and unappeased away;
She rose alone, even as alone they slept,
Nor knew what thankless vigil had been kept.
Proud was the fortress, strong the citadel,
Jealous the girl and kept her treasure well,
But thorniest flowers are pulled and even the fortress
    fell.

At that time in the town the custom was
Early on May Day through the gate to pass, .
Maidens and youths in amity together,
To go upon the hillside and to gather
Dew-heavy may and what else flowers might be
Hidden in brakes or flaunting on the tree.
With these they hung the houses and the day
Was spent in country feasting and in play,
Hiding and Seeking, Kissing in a Ring,
Here is a Thing and a very Pretty Thing,
Or Who's Your True Love Now? And when they played
At suchlike pastimes, every holdback maid
Blushed but grew kinder and grew rosy warm
And sighing leaned upon her lover's arm ;
All but the proudest beauty must relent
And yield herself in fee of that day's merriment.
But the expected hour, which all the year
Lit Helen's lovers like a beacon clear,
Found her so chilly yet that she went out
Unpartnered in the happy pairing rout
Or kept a girl on either side of her,
Or mixed so gaily in the march and stir
That none of the young men could find a place
To be sole gazer on her laughing face,
To speak aside with her in trembling tones
Or dare in love what only love condones,

The lawless hand's caress or wanton speeches,
Wherewith the suitor claims what he beseeches.
They went out singing through the portal wide
And past the runnel at the meadow-side,
The mill-wheel's clean and bubbling freshet, where
Long water-weeds hung out their trailing hair,
Past the deep mill-pool, green and dark and still,
That threw them back their pictures, past the mill
And up the lane, where first the climb began
And down the chalky ruts clear gushes ran.
Now by the roadside came the shining water,
Now went from hedge to hedge with muffled laughter
And spread across the path and stopped the way;
Then there was mocking and assumed dismay,
And lifted skirts and fearful steps and some
Were borne across but Helen would not come
A gift to any helping arm. She leapt
As lightly over as the young men stepped,
Standing a moment poised upon the edge.
Have you not seen upon the grassy ledge
Beside a pool, a slender lily swaying
At every turn of wind and each obeying,
As though in mind to leap it? Thus she stood
Under the first green shadows of the wood.

But now through scattered trees and luminous shade
Of lighter leaves they saw the open glade

94

Upon, the hill-top, where light harebells grew
Flecking the open turf with airy blue.
The troop dispersed and running up and down
Broke boughs and gathered flowers to hang the town ;
These in their baskets garnered violets new
And fresh anemones that sparkle through
The wood's light shade and glimmer in green air,
Those threaded daisies or on darkest hair
Laid garlands of the azure bells that fade
And still refuse to be light trophies made
Or grace a dwelling or exist an hour
On maiden bosoms sweeter than the flower
But sink in death away and cheat the stronger power.
Now Helen laid smooth hands upon a branch
That broke and hid her in an avalanche
Of trembling green and red. She tossed away
To waiting lads the mute and captive spray
And went where blossoms of the starry white
Nodding in careless liberty upright
Presumed to mock upon the neighbouring red
That still they lifted an unconquered head.
These made her helpless prisoners, soon she went
Deep to the knees in the green wonderment
That bordered all the wood and there she found
In folds and hollows of the broken ground
By lustrous settlements and colonies

The misty milkmaids and sunny primroses ;
All these she plucked and could not have enough
But filled her skirts with bales of shining stuff.
However long and willingly they toiled,
Yet would these treasures not have been despoiled,
Though they had harvested till odorous night
And sought for shutting blooms by glow-worm light ;
But now the sun, well risen in the sky,
Shone on the osier baskets trembling high,
And bade them homeward. So they took the way,
Mindful what yet was due of mirth and play ;
And as they travelled happy songs were sung,
Maidens and men in company, all young,
All that brave youth together, all the young !

How excellent is youth and April blood,
That is by every diverse fancy wooed
And moves as easily and merrily
As April breezes in a hawthorn-tree !
How good youth found that day to love devoted,
Well in his calendar with red marks noted,
A stage of time, a milestone in the year,
Whereby nought sad or evil came anear
But only careless joy and joyous things,
Events of mark and golden happenings !

Yet in the town was one with whom the day
Unnoticed and unhonoured burnt away,
Who lay so deep in dusty dreams and care
He had not known that May's first dawn was there.
Young Michael, for his woe, inherited
Strange figured folios from his father dead,
That set him seeking for a dismal truth
And cast a shadow early on his youth;
For though not thirty of his years were done
He lived and worked and ate and slept alone,
Renouncing every sweet companionship
And every bond of heart and hand and lip
For those uncouth and more than doubtful spells,
Whereof he sought to tame the obstinate syllables.
Long he would sit with painful, swimming eyes
On herbals and black-letter mysteries,
Or drowse himself in black and sleepy smoke
From crystal crucibles, whence he awoke
With aching forehead and with trembling limbs,
Searching the lore that swelled the unholy seraphims.
Outside his window grew a little tree
That was not propped or pruned but, blossoming free,
Knocked all that morning on the dusty pane
Its dear beseeching flowers to him in vain.
He saw it not and even smelt it not
But plunged in thornier thickets of dark thought

Pursued in heat through mental bog and briar
A phantom quarry, a Jack o' Lantern fire,
Soiling in those foul roads his youthful spirit
To gain a doubtful prize of little merit.
When noon with burning hand was come and gone
And lower stooped and lower the unhasting sun
In regular departure and the day
Fruitless for him had almost passed away,
Slant through his window came a radiance
That flickered on his books in careless dance,
Dazzling his eyes and teaching novel lust
For pastime to the grey and learned dust.
He laid aside the worm-worn manuscript,
Whence bitter honey painfully he sipped,
Marking his place with one brown finger. Still!
What music ranted from the distant hill
And moved the valley air to murmur sweet,
Breathing unwonted perfume in the street,
As though a golden light a golden sound should meet
And marry their vibrations in the air,
Nor light nor sound, but like the lucky pair
Salmacis and her lover, joined to grow more fair!
That music filled his heart with new unease;
Gazing he saw amid the lower trees ·
With unbelieving eyes a happy throng,
That ran downhill in exultation strong,

Holding aloft great branches of the may
And casting countless blossoms by the way.
Still as he gazed they grew; no more they seemed
Fantastic shapes at drowsy midnight dreamed
But breathing flesh of mortal excellence
And bodies to be seized by human sense.
Michael awoke; the new blood in his veins
Roused, like the gush of early summer rains,
A thirsty channel into busy growth
Till blossoming joy took root in obscure sloth
And green and burgeoning desires arose,
Sweet as the rose and thornier than the rose!
A day will come in studious life, when he
Who pawns youth's heritage for the rusty key
To chambers full of learning's grimy treasure
Pauses and longs to know a cleaner pleasure;
So Michael found in half a moment's time
That all his empty years were out of rhyme
With his green age and widowed of delight
His tedious day and single pillowed night.
Then in a trance he stood and wondering
Heard nearer to his house again the maidens sing,
Whereat his senses started and he knew
What to his five and twenty years was due
That yet was never paid. He cast adown
Book, crucible and tattered magic gown

And ran into the street with eyes aflame
As on their road the May Day revellers came,
Flushed with the spoil and treasure of the year
And crowned and garlanded with scented gear.
They checked their onward course and stared at him,
Being so light and gay and he so grim ;
He seemed with inky hands and matted curls
A gnarled tree in a field of flowerlike girls,
A shaggy comet in a starry night,
So blazed his eyes and so his hair upright
Circled his head with dark and waving flame,
So dusky red he grew in diffidence and shame.
They swirled in stream about, but Helen stayed
Under his glance, erect and unafraid,
And seeing her, he thought that he could see
His fortune in her bright proximity,
All kindliness and innocence and truth
And all the comeliness of living youth.
She laughed at him : O Michael—for your name
I know, and something of your dusty fame—
Will you come with us till the day be spent ?
But hearing her so light and insolent,
He felt a strange unrest, a foolish fire
Light in his heart's tough wood and rise and twire,
Flickering in the tempest of his blood
But burning still the hard and stubborn wood,

Till longing made a fury of sparks and heat
That blinded him and, swaying on his feet,
He kissed her mouth and broke in a panic away
With eyes of fear and breathing of dismay.
She panted too; the rest were silent, till
A girl behind sent up a mocking trill
Of thin clear laughter and all their laughter broke,
Louder and louder. He woke and Helen woke;
He was dying back from frenzy and she stood
Whitefaced in anger but with troubled blood;
He stammered, she said nought. Then at the last
The youths behind were eager to be past
And pushed their careless way by Michael's house,
Leaving him staring and inglorious,
Forgetful of the studies that had been
So long his spirit's solely loved demesne,
His precious drops and powders and the fume
That still with hard, stale savour filled his room.
Therein he now amazed in drowsy fit
Sought to bring back to hand his wayward wit,
That journeyed in a new and cloudier clime,
As though by drugs translated, whither time
Will years upon the perfect minute stay
Or cram a coloured lifetime in a day.
Long there he sat in revery and long

IOI

Sought to forget he had heard any song,
So all might be as erst, but found the charm too strong.

Meanwhile the gay, vociferous multitude
Awoke the town with clamorous prelude;
Joy's drums in all the ardent voices rolled
And echoed deafening from the houses cold;
The tall and silent elm-trees on the green,
That edged the street, bowed loftily their serene
Great heads, and yews in gardens walled around
Shook stiffly but responsive to the sound.
Then all the houses woke and doors were thrown
Wide open, that the music might be blown
Through the low rooms and cool wide passages
To leave behind a sweet and subtle trace
In faint-flowered curtains and old padded chairs
And, lingering at the dark turn of the stairs
Where children falter going up to bed,
Endure with homely scent to ease their dread.
The town took back its youth again, as though
A golden river on grey sand should flow
And drew them here and there and parcelled out
In house and church and hall the laden rout
To strew their gifts. And now the happy night
Drew near to them already, vaguely bright,

With longed-for victories and promised joys,
That morning pledged amid the sun and noise,
In darkness and in silence to be fulfilled,
When the lanthorns paled and the loud pipes were stilled.

But Helen was not with them. In her room,
Close curtains drawn, she brooded in the gloom
That could alone her angry roses hide
Or the white blossoms of her shaken pride
And where unheard she could both sigh and weep,
Thinking by this to lull her shame to sleep.
But all in vain, since she could not forget
What had been seen of all, the kiss that yet
Burnt on her pallid mouth and printed there
A stain that weeping could not all outwear.
So from her sighing she at last arose :
Again upon her cheeks the insulted rose
Burst into strange and sudden blossoming
And now her anger spread a rapid wing.
This is the tale of smutchèd innocence,
That, whatsoe'er the injury or whence,
She half detects a felon in her breast
And deems her enemy the fault hath guessed
And so, twice angered and with double fire,
Rebukes him in her own, her traitorous desire.

Her lamp, being lit, gave her no comfort new,
But shone too clearly out and sent all through
The shadows of her small and quiet room
A tempered radiance and a golden gloom
That, falling on her fingers, let her see
How, clenched and tight, they trembled piteously.
Ask not how she, being gentle and so young,
Could in her virgin thoughts have that among
Which now she fostered to a bitter fruit,
For shame in honest minds is oft the root
Of evil things. Who knows what storms they are
That blot out suddenly the sailor's star
Of peace in his own soul? They rise unbidden
From distant seas and icy mountains hidden
Far off in lands untraversed. Reason then
Drives blindly on till calm returns again,
Nor guesses whither but despairingly
Gives up the rudder to the tyrant sea
And shuddering hears the hard-tried timbers start
In that fine ship she navigates—the heart.
So, anger being master, Helen took
The yellow flyleaf of an ancient book
And wrote in haste what words she had to write,
Nor would not read them through but quickly doused the
    light,

And ran with panting bosom down the stair
To find unseen her chosen messenger.
She sent him off and fled in haste again
To hide from all her mingled fear and pain
And to determine, if much brooding might,
What end should come at last to that eventful night.

A garden underneath her window lay
That in the cool and breathless end of day
Sent up sharp perfumes climbing to her sill
To take the shadowy air by waves and fill
Her room with ghosts of flowers. The lane below
Lay empty, but the town was louder now
With silver quiring and with wanton cries,
That ever in a maddening strain would rise,
Clearer and stronger, till the troubled air
Streamed in a turmoil and the lights aglare
Laid out before the gust their long and tossing hair.
All this she heard and saw, and she could see
Her young companions go by two and three
Across the lane's dark entry, where the grass
Grew in the flags, whereat a faint : Alas !
Rose in her bosom, neither willed nor owned,
But still by hotter spite to be atoned.
And yet the lane below unvisited
Lay silent till the quick, triumphant tread

Of Michael sounded there, whose happy eyes
Looked upward in a certain lover's guise ;
For him her messenger had found alone,
Drowsing in dulness, by his black hearthstone,
And given him her letter, which, being read,
Set the swift blood a-spinning in his head.
Then he had risen and with care had drest,
And niceness, that the beating heart confessed,
And gone to keep the tryst, as fine as one
Could be who never yet on love's wild ways had run.
He passed amid the gay and careless crowd,
As little noticed as a midnight cloud,
And heard no syllable of all their song
That shook the dusky trees and died in long
Reverberations down the alleys deep
Where workday tools forgotten lay asleep ;
He passed the lighted windows where the old
Amused the night with stories manifold
And bragging legends of their days of gold ;
He passed young daring girls, who mocked him after
And loosed light arrows from the bow of laughter ;
He passed them in a lonely happiness
And turned into the dark lane's quiet recess.
Then Helen waiting saw him come and set
A candle in her window. Through the wet

And odorous hedge, he ran towards the sign,
Coming out wreathed with tangled trail and vine,
Convolvulus and creeping briony,
And stood before her garlanded. But she,
Leant down to him and whispered through the still
Sharp-scented air that lay upon her sill
A word of honeyed consequence, wherein
His name afloat, like flowers in heady wine,
Enchanted him to stammering and threw
His sense unguarded from the level true.
How shall I come to you, sweet love? he cried.
But she with finger on her lip replied:
Hush! for the night is young and all awake,
And none must know how we our secret pleasure take.
What should I do if any found you here?
You are too loud a lover. O, I fear
Lest in your eagerness you should proclaim
To all at once your triumph and my shame;
In silence take what secretly is given,
Nor shout your victory to the listening heaven,
But breathe it on my breast and I shall hear
What could not be so sweet cried in the loud mob's ear.
How shall I come to you, he cried again,
Softer, since love in him did love restrain,
Whereto she answered: You shall say, not I;
Can wizards not by incantation fly

Astride a slip of thorn ? But in despair
He raised his wild arms up and said to her :
My craft avails me not, for I have learnt
No gallant's tricks like these. I never burnt
Till now to climb a maiden's window nor
Studied the cantraps some have made therefor.
What shall I do ? Must we the whole night long
Gaze at a distance ? Surely I am strong
And I will climb to you or find a way. . . . .
He ceased and no word further could he say,
Being by love made dumb and made a fool,
Such as he is who is just escaped from wisdom's rule.
But while in misery his body shook
Helen adjured him with a merry look
And said she had not brought him there in vain
To see her window and go home again,
And thereupon let down to him a great
Basket, that had through half the year for freight
The wizened winter-apples, packed away
And growing sweeter and fewer every day,
But now must hold a heavier load instead,
A lover going to a lawless bed.
I'll draw you up in this, she breathed ; but he
Looked at the height and stood uncertainly
Doubting her strength, until she laughed again :
Love pulls the rope with me and halves the pain,

And night is wasting, Michael, and I have made
An easy pulley for my better aid.
Come, if you truly love me ! He thereat
Hastily in the swinging basket sat,
And as she drew he dug his nails between
The wall's great stones a little way to win,
And as she laboured he bore double strain
Till all his muscles ached with twice her pain,
And double agony his heart possessed
To hear the loud breath in her toiling breast
And think that she should stiffen every limb
And tax her blood to give herself to him.

Much ere he came in thoughts that hurried past,
She mused what she must do with him at last,
And in perplexity had put aside
Her many plans for taking down his pride
And still had made no plan ; but when he came
So close to her, his eyes revived her shame
And sent new anger running in her breast,
For now his foolish heart, by hope caressed,
Moved him to praise her in a voice that shook
And stare on her with so possessive look
And glance so greedy and assured that he
Burnt up at once her doubtful leniency.

Are you spent, love? he asked her, being aware
That now the basket rocked in middle air,
Tie up the rope and rest. But she replied:
Rest easy, Michael, for the rope is tied
And we are safe together, you and I.
Therewith, into the room's obscurity,
She disappeared and silence settled down
On that one alley in the noisy town.
When she had gone, he lay awhile at ease,
Whispering fondly inward foolishness,
How lovely she was, how made for him to adore
With that young heart which never loved before,
How high a spirit and what a gallant fire
Had leapt impetuous to his desire,
How her mind marched with his against delay
And tumbled all the barriers from the way!
He sighed in the darkness, smiled and was content,
Nor cared at first how long the minutes went
Brushing his face with slow, enchanted wings
And filling his mind with magical new things,
He lay so close to all he coveted
That love cried truce and reason, lightly sped,
Entered upon a new and drowsy reign,
Wherein there was no movement nor no pain,
But honeyed longing that without a smart
Brims up the intricate vessel of the heart,

And promised happiness that lighter lies
Than rose-petals on the most burning eyes.
Long he lay motionless in such a trance,
But acrid fire began again to advance
And stung him, that he had not heard above
A new beginning of the toils of love,
Nor words of joy nor any promises,
Which as the gift itself the unpractised lover please.
Then in that stillness fear got room to throw
A panic in his heart and check the flow
Of the delighted blood ; one dark thought sped
From heart to hands : What if the girl were dead,
Slain by the labour that for love she bore ?
Michael leapt up ; the basket trembled sore,
Yet sorer shook his limbs, and as he stared,
Darkness replied above and he despaired.

While thus he languished in his bitterness
Behind his back a murmur 'gan to press
From the singing far away, towards the lane,
Strayed echoes of the festival refrain
That louder grew until the very sound
Did from the high and shadowy walls rebound
And wake him from the stupor, so that he
Turning beheld the alley suddenly

Filled with a shouting mob, whose torches flung
Light in the dark air, where amazed he hung,
And in whose web of interwoven noise
He heard first one and then another voice,
That cried his name aloud and bade him climb
The further way nor longer wait on time
But of himself to assure felicity.
Then, at the cawing of that rookery,
Blood filled his splitting brain, his burning eyes
Darkened and swelled, he felt his arteries
Straining and giving and his hands clenched tight
Upon the swaying rope. But still the light
Derisive roar pleased itself below,
Numbing his brain in his pride's overthrow.
He would have fled them, but he could not flee,
Would have ignored them, yet could not but see,
Till at the last anger possessed him too
And pride returned and courage from them grew,
And, turning on the crowd, he would have spoken
But by the noise beneath his words were broken,
Thrown high and scattered in the silent night
That lay acalm above the crowd's delight.
Silence! he cried again. His mockers still
Derided him, men loud and women shrill,
But the third time he used such vehemence,
Such thunder in his voice and so immense

A gesture of his spread and threatening hand
That all grew quieter, as the poplars stand
Whispering between the onslaughts of the storm,
And stared like fools upon his swaying form.
Then in that silence mightily he said :
I will be gentle, though about my head
Your brutal mockeries spin and though I see
The trick the wanton girl has played on me.
I will be gentle. Helen ! make an end,
Lest I should do what you can never mend.
Free me and let me down. A quietness fell,
Wherein the trees' low sigh was audible
And nothing else. He heard no sound above,
No sign of her repentance or her love ;
The rope hung still and taut. But now beneath,
First came a whisper, then a rising breath,
And lastly uproar, wherein no word was,
But as the wind and wave contend in tongueless cause.
But that great crying fell as it began ;
From group to yelling group a silence ran
And laid a finger on the mouths that cried
Till in low murmurings the tumult died
And Michael spoke again, slow, heavy words,
That floated through the hush like ominous birds.
I have not learnt, he said, the trivial spell
That can a woman's mutinous heart compel.

But I who am weak in dealing with desire
Can yet constrain earth, water, air and fire,
And, for this town hath mocked me and since one
Hath hurt me closer than all your taunts have done,
I make return ! Henceforth no fire shall live
Within your houses and the fugitive
Light flame that dances in your lanthorns shall
To blackened nothing in an instant fall.
You elements, with whom I dwelt at ease,
Come to my aid, confound mine enemies !
Out, friendly light and warmth ! Out, every flame !
Back to the yokeless aether whence ye came !

Thereon a strange and dizzying thing befell
For, quicker than the magic takes to tell,
While still they gaped, they suddenly were aware
How from their torches into the still air
The bright fire slipped and instantly was gone,
Like burning-plumaged coveys, journeying on
From human haunts to fabled Araby.
They gazed about and everywhere could see
The shining casements blackened and gone blind,
And in that lightless waste no man could find
His neighbour or his friend. Then down they threw
Their useless lanthorns and the panic grew;

The weaker cried and wailed with piteous voice
And the dark lane re-echoed with the noise
Of broken men and women, whose dismay
Spared not each other as they fled away
From Michael's wrath and left him hanging there.
And now, with dreadful whisperings, despair
Ran through the town, as erst the darkness ran,
And laid on every house its gloomy ban ;
Flint lost its virtue and the friendly flame
Lay in the pebble whence before it came ;
There was no moon, the stars were faint and few
And still the dreadful night was hardly half-way through.

Then in a pitiful agony hurried all
To that dark shadow hanging on the wall
And begged with breaking voices and loud sighs
That he would turn on them compassionate eyes
And give them back again their patron flame.
They knelt to him and prayed and felt no shame,
And sobbed and stormed at him in unison :
But when their maudlin beggary was done,
He answered coldly : What you now entreat
Cheaply you valued, when you deemed it meet
To mock one greater than your hearts have known.
Suffer together now, as I alone,

And have the heart to be as silent as I,
Lest I should turn on you my mockery.
They answered him : We are humble, we are broken,
We kneel to you and offer you as token
Our outstretched hands and bended heads and ask
That you will set on us some heavy task
To prove our single heart. But he replied :
Were I to yield, your tears would not be dried,
The dust be hardly scattered from your knees
Ere you would charm away your promises
More easily than I your lanthorns quelled.
A deep low groan from all that concourse welled
And sank again in harsh and sullen sound,
Like lost winds on a waste and barren ground.
Dumbly they waited ; silently he stood,
Raised as a judge upon that multitude ;
Sound slept and time stood still ; neither he nor they
Knew how far night had gone along her way
Before he spoke again : O little creatures,
That dare not face the night, without all nature's
Coddling and cherishing and friendliness
But catch affrighted at her swinging dress
For warmth and shelter and as little know
Herself as the dumb beasts that creeping go,
I'll stand no more between you and your nurse ;
A little thing shall take away my curse.

When I have ended what is here begun
And my long journey up the wall is done,
And I have taken what is promised me,
Once more in torch and lanthorn burning free
The gallant flame shall scare this cold inanity!
All shuddered and none spoke; their whispering
Moved in the darkness like a living thing,
A tense and deeply breathing animal
That could through tight and trembling bodies crawl
And draw existence from their agony.
From no man's throat, and yet from all, a cry
Rose thinly up and offered him his will
With their submission. But he heard them still
With scorn and answered not. And Helen lying
Hid in her chamber mused upon that crying,
How once these maddened men were hers to rule
And each before her stood an equal fool,
Stammered when she spoke and simpered at her smile
And sought with tedious homage to beguile
Her heart impregnable. She could not hear
Their vows below for cold and sickening fear
That drowned her spirit, yet, in that forlorn
Deep night, a sudden doubtful star was born,
A flickering spark she scarcely could descry
That moved and winked and cheated still her eye,

And yet at last, the more she thought thereon,
With steady and with friendly radiance shone ;
For she imagined in that dreadful hour
An iron courage and a golden power
And Michael standing over all the crowd,
Strong as they weak and quiet as they loud.
She saw nought else but this ; she did not see
A trembling and a ruffian two or three
That came to draw the too long idle rope
And grin at her from time to time, in hope
Through the thick shade to see her blushing deep
Or hear her praying them or hear her weep.
Her thoughts were what the tree's are, when the
    wind
Strips the light petals off and leaves the fruit behind.

Outside they saw with hot and starting eyes
Slow in the dark the heavy basket rise
And saw a shadow from the shadow climb
And slip into the casement. Tardy time
Stood still again and so immense a hush
Reigned in the town that an uneasy bush
Rubbing its boughs together seemed as though
A mighty storm in mighty trees did blow ;
So long the moment was that men believed
Night's cog was slipped or time's old hour-glass thieved,

That day's sweet advent was for ever past
And that the rolling world was stayed at last.
Then one cried : Look ! and all together cried,
For this man in his lanthorn light had spied
And that had seen a blackened kitchen-fire
Glow faintly into crimson and expire
And glow again. Then in a rush of light
The gabled houses stood out tall and bright,
Lit by a lucid flood that overshone
All that the human eye can gaze upon,
Nor could they lift their lids again to see
Until it sank in peaceful radiancy.
And then a glow ineffably serene,
Sleeping on every torch and wick was seen,
A friendly light, so friendly, that a strange
Beatitude, a soft and melting change,
Soothed the wild heart and filled the uneasy breast
With golden hopes of joy and silver hopes of rest.

THE QUEEN OF CHINA; A POEM

" How we spun
A shroud of talk to hide us from the sun
Of this familiar life."

CHARACTERS

The King.

The Prince.

The General.

The Chamberlain.

Two Italian Travellers.

An Old Scholar.

Three Doctors.

A Young Courtier.

Two Sentries.

The Prince's Servant

The Queen.

Two Slave Girls.

A Girl's Voice.

Place. Various parts of the Royal Palace of China.

Time. In the Fourteenth Century of the Christian Era.

FIRST ACT

FIRST ACT

Courtyard of the Royal Palace in the capital of China.
Enter the KING *and the* GENERAL.

GENERAL.

You are in haste, my lord?

KING.

I still must haste
To catch the light before it flies from me,
And now the council gathers. You are called:
Will you not come?

GENERAL.

I have despatches.

KING.

Well?

To read in council?

GENERAL.

Ours alone at first,
Not to be judged on hastily nor thrown

Unthought on to the common ear, so grave,
So large with menace are their languages
And yet so full of chance. . . .

KING.

Of chance? Speak on;
I listen.

GENERAL.

These are from the Tartar border
Where now the wretched villages in flame
Prophesy woe to come with smoky tongues.
The foe is out,
His army largely set and ravaging
Our lands unshielded. Up and down the marches
Our scanty soldiers move in desperate packs
And hold their line with peril.

KING.

And the army?
Are all our troops at move?

GENERAL.

An hour ago
I set our messengers on every road.

The governors are stirring to the work,
My missives dropping in the cantonments
Inflame their hearts already. Have no fear
Nor doubt success. We'll push them back again
Until their host in ruin overtopples
Like a young foolish horse that rears and falls,
Crushing his rider under him. We'll have them down.

KING.

Why, this is well.

GENERAL.

And yet not well enough.
For now we may with just excuse and much
Indulgence of our purpose scald the sore
That festers in our side. I'd raise an army,
More than the border hath these twenty years
Trembled beneath the tread of. Then their land
Shall lie unfended from our blow and crouch
Beaten and bloody, begging clemency,
And offer tribute as a recompense
And be a province.

KING.

These are weary schemes
And bloody projects and we two are old.
Our days in the field are done, our lances much

Out of the fashion and our banners set
Below the newer time. Vain words to me !
A speech for younger soldiers—for my son.

GENERAL.

Your son. . . .

KING.

You speak with such a heavy tongue
The two reluctant syllables, your mouth
Trembles, your eyes avoid my eyes—

GENERAL.

Your son. . . .

KING.

What would you say then ?

GENERAL.

My dear lord, you know—

KING.

My son's not whole, my son is heavy and sick.
He hath a dropsy of thought, his swoln affections
Clog him and hamper him. I know it all.
I have observed him and you observing him ;

Often the same thoughts lay in our two brains,
By silence and by shame dissevered. Gladly
I'd give an army to him for the toy
That princely youth delights in.

GENERAL.

O dear Lord!
Stands it on this? Must we attend his sickness?
Will you not take the battle for an ease
Of all your care in watching over him?

KING.

I am too old
And age hath sucked my plenitude of desire;
The vessels are dried up,
Wherein the hot and maddening lymph resided
That urges men to conquest. This will be
A mighty war for glory and renown—
You speak an ancient tongue, a dialect
My lips have lost the use of. I have known
Glory, the toy that young men die to purchase,
Gilded with blood and cried up with men's groans,
An object of desire, a precious taste,
But I've no relish in it, being old.
If my son's blood were young as are his years. . . .

GENERAL.

Wise huntsmen sometimes take an ailing hound
Out to the coursing-places that he knew
And let him scent the quarry for a cure.

KING.

Well like a huntsman spoken !

GENERAL.

          He that knows
Nature of dog and horse is wise enough
To govern many men.

KING.

          Is this not he,
That slowly walks along the avenue ?
Speak with him warily. I'll try your cure
And trust your skill in venery. Here he comes.

(The PRINCE *enters.)*

PRINCE.

I wish you happiness, dear father.

KING.

          And I
Wish you more spirit and a cheerful look
To front the morning with.

GENERAL.

Good prince, brave youth,
Are you a youth indeed or older than we ?
For on your brow anticipating age
Hath traced his plot of ground and marked his jointure
Before his claim's allowed by natural sense
Or any judgement.

PRINCE.

I am sad, I own,
And look not brightly out nor think not bravely.

KING.

What ails you then ?

PRINCE.

Why, sir, I cannot tell
What strange infection spreads along my veins
And drowses in my heart. I am not sick,
Not fevered, coughing, palsied, none of these,
Nor visited with pain. O, let me rest,
For my disease hath touched the will of youth
To be at work and, were my labour done
In sixty heavy years, I could not be
More weary or more out of love with life
And lifeless in my love.

133

KING.

What, boy, you love?

PRINCE.

Only the world and what therein doth stand
I counted formerly, as lovers count
Their mistresses' most delicate delights,
But earth no longer pleases my dull eyes.
Let me alone, most gracious lord, for this
Is but a male green-sickness, want of blood
That duly not performs its proper task
To feed the passions.

GENERAL.

When you carried arms
And sat your horse and led your troop, you looked not
So faintly mooded. You were strong of hand
And sometimes I could see your parted lips
Whisper a silent song to company you
In time with the horse's gallop. We have ridden,
Where the dim morning struggled with the mist
On the wide plain, before the ranked army,
Galloping side by side and marshalling
The fiery soldiers. You were happy then,
Quick to command and rapid in your sight,
And no disease fretted your body thus

134

With cruel teeth to make an ornament
Of woe and stricken flesh. O come with me,
For there's adventure yet and troops to lead
And smoke and dust to snuff where men contend.

PRINCE

I have forgotten all you speak of now.

GENERAL.

The Tartars insolently ride their horses
Over the ash of our burnt villages !

KING.

If arms could win my son from his disease,
I'd make a war for medicine and reckon
The ravaged border but a blister set
To draw the kingdom's humours.

PRINCE.

Dear my lord,
King reverenced, father loved, and both obeyed
With all humility and all affection,
If I am slow in taking up the word
That now you cast to me, I have no fear.
I would not set one penny on my life

135

Nor take a step aside from waiting death :
But I am spiritless and ill at ease
And would not wear my mail nor sit my horse.
I am sick, I am sick and will not touch the lance
Nor lift the sword nor set my foot in stirrup
But still with drooping head and unlit face
Go pacing on my ways about the court
And let the months run by uncounted still.

GENERAL.

May the gods give you a more morning mood
And something better rising in your heart.
You were not so.

KING.

Nor I, when I was young.

GENERAL.

No, by the gods ! You were a lusty boy,
Save when a lady flouted you. Shame upon you,
Dear prince, to languish so without a cause !
No wound, no ailment nor no hurt of love
Can you advance in reason. You confess
That you have borne a thin and general love
To all creation and dispersed your heart
Unthriftily on the world and thus you are sick

Of mere philosophy. Man, love your horse
And tend your arms and cherish one beside,
A lady, any lady, and be glad
A soldier wants so little to be glad.

PRINCE.

I am no soldier, I !
I find no sweetness in the emulation
Of giving death or braving it.
Count me an emptied man, a youthful dotard,
Who totters down his early years and fades
Out of the bright-aired places that he knew,
Too dull to be regretful. So's my humour,
Still to be sad, still to be unaroused,
And let my passions rot or rest in peace.

GENERAL.

But hear what's now on foot. A moment yet !
You have not understood.

KING.

           We cannot move him.
I dreamt—we both were foolish. Let it pass
And let the years have sway. In his high season,
Fair unadorned youth will scare these mists
And show himself with burning face arisen

137

Over the astonished country ere we die.
I'll leave unstirred the waters of my grief:
These arguments are like the wands wherewith
Boys puddle in a stagnant pool and raise
Bubbles of nauseous air, from slime corrupted,
That chokes the heart with sickness. Did I linger
Too much on this or think it past all hope,
The happiness that fills my flowing days
Were poisoned at the root. O, plead no more!

(*Enter the* CHAMBERLAIN.)

CHAMBERLAIN.

Great king, the dragon-throne is set
And ringed with all your guards in golden mail.
The reverend mandarins are crowding in
And lose their several wisdoms in the crowd
With pushings, stampings and revilings. Now
The Queen is on her way.

KING.

                    Come, my old friend;
My son, your place, though dumb, is at my side.

PRINCE.

My place in council suits well with my mind,
For there the young are licensed to be dumb.

GENERAL.

This is a damnable virtue in a youth
To obey so readily what age prescribes.
Youth should be chidden and give cause to chide ;
Iron's not forged except it glowing be.

KING.

Let us go in, old fellow. Youth refuses
The high adventure we have offered it.
There are no wars now, swords are out of fashion.

(They go in. Two SENTRIES *take up their posts at the gate.)*

1ST SENTRY.

There are wars going. Did you hear the general ?

2ND SENTRY.

I heard something. I heard two old men bewailing their age and that they might not lead us youngsters to be killed like willing horses under their palsied legs. Make no account of it all but lean on your pike, my lad, and take it easy. The pike is wood and we flesh, it senseless and we weary ; let it do our work.

139

Stand up to your work, you crook-backed soldier. The wooden shaft will feel the serjeant's cane more kindly than your shoulders, if he finds you stooping on guard, like an old man mending a shoe.

2ND SENTRY.

You are wise and witty and pretty and smutty and full of good advice.

1ST SENTRY.

Look! there's a shadow coming through the doorway.

2ND SENTRY.

Stand where you are or I'll stick you!

(*The Two* TRAVELLERS *enter*.)

1ST SENTRY.

Not like that! Is that language for the king's guard? Halt where you stand, strangers, and give me an account of yourselves or you shall taste affliction.

2ND SENTRY.

Very noble! Very praiseworthy! Do but stick them in so formal a manner and they will die in the politest agony.

140

1st Traveller.

We are known, good soldier, we are customed here :
Let us but one step further in to find
Good friends and many.

2nd Sentry.

Not a step.' You have such villainous brown faces as if
you had been overbaked in hell, and such sharp long noses
that you might have bored your way out of the oven therewith. And you have round eyes, not like ours.

1st Traveller.

We are foreigners

And yet not enemies.

2nd Traveller.

Stand off, young fool,

Whom half a month of half-learnt drill hath taught
To tyrannise and threaten with the pike,
That trembles in your clumsy fingers.

1st Traveller.

Still !

Enough of quarrelling words. Good soldier, go
And fetch the ancient Chamberlain, whom we knew.
His warrant will suffice to stamp us friendly
And worthy of admission.

2ND SENTRY.

I'll go. I know the Chamberlain and I'll stretch my legs
looking for him. Hold them off, comrade, put your pike
at their bellies and entertain them with pleasant words.
I'll be a messenger.

(*He goes out.*)

1ST SENTRY.

Stay where you are, gentlemen, or in all kindliness I
must prick you. I bear you no ill will, I am your most
obedient servant, but if you move a step, I'll let your
blood.

2ND TRAVELLER.

A courteous cut-throat !

1ST TRAVELLER.

See, the Chamberlain
Approaches, almost hasting !

(*The* CHAMBERLAIN *enters.*)

Do you know us ?
Do our countenances in your memory hold
Or hath not amity such preserving stuff
To keep our pictures constant in your eyes ?

CHAMBERLAIN.

I know you not. . . . I know you ! Is it true ?
You are here again, old friends ?

1ST TRAVELLER.

After long leagues
On camel-back across the bitter sands
That are more salt than is the merciless sea
And not so beautiful.

CHAMBERLAIN.

But you are here,
New washed and cleanly clothed, with happy faces,
Among your ancient though your alien friends.

2ND TRAVELLER.

We have come to you again, I know not why,
For surely there is joy in Lombardy ;
The clear white wine is made there and the women
Are also clear and white and straight and tall
And the grey olives grow upon the hills
In sunshine no less generous than this.
But we have ridden on horses, mules and camels
And crossed wide seas in many dangerous ships
To be with you again.

1ST TRAVELLER.

                     Is there no news ?
Or is the kingdom still as when we left it,
Placid and sleepy and daily growing fat
On the rich harvest of the river-mud ?
Have not the Tartars once come down like hail
To rumple the silk skirts of your fair women
And slay your wise men in their libraries ?

CHAMBERLAIN.

You have gone and come again as to your home
After a day of absence. Still the river
Leaves its deposit on the layered shore
And there the corn and soft green rice-stalks grow
Each year in greater plenty, maize and millet
Choke up the fields and block the winding valleys
In wealthiest abundance. Still the people
Are placid, sleepy and have every day
More than is time enough to sun themselves
Outside the doorways of their light-built houses.
All these things are the same. Go you about
And look for what is changed in any street
And you'll not find one house built or pulled down.

2ND TRAVELLER.

And the court ?

144

CHAMBERLAIN.

The court—aye, there a change might be,
For peoples change not but a king grows old
And alters love and chooses better friends
To guide his counsel or delight his heart.
The old king dies and burns his life away
Daily like a glowing ember in a draught :
The keen air of youth's passionate ideas
Blows through his aged brain and fans it up
Into consuming fire.

2ND TRAVELLER.

He is lunatic ?
Is that what you would say ?   An old man mad ?
Perhaps he has a new wife in his bed
And wastes his scanty breath in loving her.

CHAMBERLAIN.

He has taken a new wife into his house
And yet his hands have not unloosed her girdle,
So much he holds her high in reverence.

1ST TRAVELLER.

A new queen wears the crown, the king's a lover !
And gone back fifty years in boyishness

L   145

Sickly to glance upon a maiden's zone !
On with your news ; discourse !

CHAMBERLAIN.

    O beauty long
Has never lightened these dim walks and ways,
But now she dwells among us as a queen
And holds her court with us.

1ST TRAVELLER.

     The old king loves
This newly planted slip of beauty, this
Stranger unheard of by the men we knew ?

CHAMBERLAIN.

He loves her and she lives alone
In the pavilion yonder by the lake,
And sleeps alone.

2ND TRAVELLER.

We come from countries where men honestly
Lie if the need be but dress up no riddles
That cloak the truth and leave its heart unchanged.
Old chamberlain, your narrow, wrinkled eyes
Perplex me.

146

1ST TRAVELLER.

Peace! the manner of these strange men
Is to conceal. We grow too old, we two,
And too much versed in our wide travelling
To cry this land up and that land down.
All peoples are bright butterflies to me,
Rejoicing me in variance. As well desire
That all the birds of the earth should sing one song
As that all men should show one face to us.

CHAMBERLAIN.

Yet have I spoken truth. The king's new wife
Is virgin still.

2ND TRAVELLER.

And you called her beauty's self?
Or is she some princess from lower China,
As stiff and ugly as the treaty-seal
Whose part she plays?

CHAMBERLAIN.

She is most beautiful.
And therefore the king mounts not her chaste bed,
Because he dares not till she beckon him.

Is he become a dotard, straitly bound
By an imaginary chain ? O sorrow !
That the great wise old king should stoop to beg
A woman's kisses in senility.

CHAMBERLAIN.

She is a slave,
·Her father's name and house alike unknown,
Her limbs and life being subject to the law,ı
To whipping, tearing, branding and the wheel
If she should disobey. A distant Viceroy,
Out of a city high among the mountains,
Sent her, a chosen gift, to please the king,
With fifty mounted men to be her guard.
They rode around her sternly with drawn swords,
She resting in their midst as easily
As doth a slight flower in a fold of the rocks
Where soil has gathered and birds dropped a seed.

.1ST TRAVELLER.

Did she, on seeing, make her lord a slave ?

CHAMBERLAIN.

She gave the king a letter and stood mute
With folded hands before the dragon-throne

148

And quiet lips and all submissive eyes.
But when he had read it and had gazed on her
He drew her to his side and on his seat
And bade her rule his courtiers, which she does
With words and glances, drawing reverence
From bearded barons and old generals.
Even the ribald young men of the court
For whom to jest is such occasion now
Hush their light tongues and gravely speak of her
With worship.

2ND TRAVELLER.

                    Do you speak to us of her,
Catalogue all her beauties and declare
Her virtues to us.

CHAMBERLAIN.

                    It was recently
You called me old,
Spoke of my narrow and my wrinkled eyes,
Too narrow, too wrinkled to let beauty in,
And age has withered up my lively tongue
That cannot now discourse of lovely things.
There are younger men than I to speak of her.

(A YOUNG COURTIER crosses the stage.)

1ST TRAVELLER (*approaching him*).

Be done with those soft dreams your eyes betray,
Young lord, and tell me what thing is the queen?

COURTIER.

She is an arrow flown against the wind.

(*He passes out.*)

2ND TRAVELLER.

The one's too cold to speak and all the rest
Too hot for reason. She's a woman doubtless
Who in the crowd of dainty courtiers
Will find a lover nearly to her choice
And make the best of him. Till then she keeps
The aged doddering king out of her bed
And by a feignèd mystery chains the court
In worship of her.

1ST TRAVELLER.

          But the king was wise
And in his veins the blood ran still and true
When last we sojourned here.

CHAMBERLAIN.

          The king is wise
But now his wisdom is a fierier sort ;

Not the tame learning of sedentary sages
But a fierce active knowledge that destroys
And feeds upon the instrument it uses.
He rises early, goes about his day
With such quick zest and uncontrolled desire
That the inmost chambers of the sacred house
Hear now a sound till this unknown to them,
Rustling of royal silks in haste that pass.

1st Traveller.

O marvellous transformation! The old grave king
Who ruled his happy kingdom soberly,
Surrounded by the gravest mandarins,
That ever China knew! I am amazed.
He will wear armour now and go to war,
Waving his sword beneath the dragon-banner,
And dream of conquest like an untaught boy.

Chamberlain.

Deem not the king is grown again a child.
He is most wise, I say, and all his passions
Are governed by a fire beyond our sight.

2nd Traveller.

Are you too fallen a slave to this strange girl?
Behind the riddle of your changeless eyes

151

I half see mysteries moving. We have known
In our own land how courts are set aflame
And princes maddened for a worthless woman
And the old tales tell, which we hold for truth,
How empires vaster than we now obey
Hung in the fingers of an idle queen,
Such power has beauty had in Italy.
But here! You cluster round your river mud
And tend the rice-crop, year on patient year,
And the grave kings succeed eternally
One to another in unbroken peace.
What should you know of love and lust and war,
Parricide, matricide, and fratricide,
Fire, rapine and the sheathless thirsty sword
And all the ills that women bring on princes?
I will not yet believe it.

1st Traveller.

How stands the prince
In this new turmoil of the wildered court,
Who when we last were here was next the throne,
His father's chosen son?

Chamberlain.

He is grown grave.
Even as the king has waxed in youthfulness,

So he in gravity and the look of years.
You were his friends before but you'll be fortuned
If now he will exchange five words with you.

2ND TRAVELLER.

The court is surely mazed.

1ST TRAVELLER.

Changed at the heart.
And yet the land as we came through it here
Slept on its old and well-remembered sleep.
The light junks glided on the yellow stream,
The country, right and left, an endless field
Of greening crops in tranquil busyness
Lay like a sleepy hive. Your working people
Stood quietly to their labour. Yet, in our absence,
Time has been busy and remorseless change
Fretting away the features of our love
And laying down strange shapes to meet our touch.
Even here the halls and gardens are the same :
I do remember that old climbing jasmin,
Whose gnarlèd roots start stiffly from the ground
In writhen nakedness but higher up
Burst in a boundless fountain of white flowers.
Here in this garden once with care you taught me

153

The secrets of your white-haired scientists,
Compass and printing-press and dreadful dust,
That being lit will blow great walls apart,
Secrets I carried back to see despised
In mine own native land, where yet they grow
—And now one secret you withhold from me.

2ND TRAVELLER.

Who is this man that walks with blackened brow
And frowning purpose? Is it the general
That swept with purifying flame the hills
Which were infect with rebels?

CHAMBERLAIN.

It is he.

2ND TRAVELLER.

Ask, ask of him.

(*The* GENERAL *crosses the stage.*)

1ST TRAVELLER.

You were my friend when first I visited
The court of China.

154

(The GENERAL *stands and stares at him.)*

       Tell, O tell me now
Who is this queen, this mystery shrouded woman
Who captivates the king and wraps up all
In a close-meshèd veil of sorcery?
Tell me, I pray you, for you are a man
In the high summer of a human life,
Ripe yet not buried in the mound of years,
Master of life, experienced in death,
Having led armies and commanded men.

     GENERAL.

She is a trumpet blowing to distant wars.

     1ST TRAVELLER.

You tell me nothing—or much.

     GENERAL.

      No more—no more.

    (He passes out.)

     2ND TRAVELLER.

Are they all mad?
    155

CHAMBERLAIN.

                The court is breaking up
And all are passing out.

2ND TRAVELLER.

                Here comes the prince
With chin reposing gravely on his breast
And his still hands folded behind his back.
I dare not speak to him.

1ST TRAVELLER.

                But I will speak
Because this mystery presses on my heart.
He is yet young, he hath not thirty years :
His icy posture is not natural
Even in a young man of this strange land.
Perhaps to see his ancient friends again
Will melt his blood for any purposes.

(*The* PRINCE *enters.*)

2ND TRAVELLER.

He is not the same as these are, for his face
Is sorrowful. Here there's no mystery.
I have not in this country seen a man

Whose countenance was marked as this man's is,
Showing what all they hide.

1st Traveller.

Beloved lord !
We are two travellers, come from the west,
To visit China once again.

Prince.

Be welcome !
The chamberlain shall wait on you.

1st Traveller.

You know us,
If but your royal memory carries back
A few years past.

Prince.

I know you, yes, I know you.

2nd Traveller.

Accept our duty, sir, and our true love,
The same love which of old we bore to you,
Which you returned, we thought.

157

PRINCE.

I do not change,
Though a slight cause may make me moody now
And scant of words. I know you well indeed ;
You are the brave Italians who came
First of your race to visit China's court,
With whom too I have held long conference,
Learning the ways of many foreigners,
As is most meet for princes so to do.
Welcome again ! You see I am uneasy
But it is nothing. Cure my ills with words,
Brave words and coloured, lit by distant suns
And blown by many winds. You are welcome here
And shall have what you will. Come you for trade ?

1ST TRAVELLER.

We come for knowledge, sir, and old affection,
And all we ask of you is also words,
News of the country and our friends herein.

PRINCE.

Of whom count me the chief, at least in kindness,
To serve you well, if not in your esteem.
I am as you see me, strong in body and heart,
In spirit unperturbed, as formerly
You knew me.

158

    And the king, your father, sir ?

PRINCE.

As well as I, with more of the look of youth
Than I can claim to. He is busier,
More anxious for the state, as years pass on,
Leaving each year a dole of wisdom with him.
He will rejoice to know his well-loved roof
Shelters two ancient friends once more. He holds it
Inalienably the duty of a king
To comfort travellers and let them go
Ready to come again. I'll send to him.

2ND TRAVELLER.

And the new queen ?

PRINCE.

    What ! you have heard of her ?
Yet she is not of the number of your friends.

2ND TRAVELLER.

Her fame has travelled through the country, sir,
And all the bumpkins in the villages,
When they speak of the wonders of the capital,
Add : And the king has taken a new wife.

PRINCE.

I cannot speak of her. She is as high
Above my praise, as my thoughts of her are higher
Than of ought else. She is a halcyon,
Born to send sunny days on China.

1st Traveller.

She

Is beautiful ?

PRINCE.

You tempt me on, good friend,
But I am slow, knowing what's out of reach,
And that's her picture to be made in words.
Had I a poet's golden phrase at call
And golden music in my voice, I could not
Depict her in her loveliness, detail
The curves of cheek and breast and archèd foot,
Explain the eyes' soft splendour.

2nd Traveller.

In our land,
Poets tell more than this and they set out
How she spreads wide her arms to take her lover,
And how her soft lips meet and answer his
Dumbly.

PRINCE.

I said no single word of love,
But only that the queen's bright excellence
Is far beyond my praise. O she is lovely
Even as a pearl new-taken from the sea :
She moves in radiance through the wildered court
And the gay silks that hide her sweetly flow
About the rhythmic motion of her easy limbs.
You know how we wake one morning here to find
Outside our opened windows the cherry-tree
Suddenly blooming. Our hearts are then amazed
And falter with the consciousness of beauty.

(*He turns half away and is silent.*)

1ST TRAVELLER (*softly*).

She is so fair, my lord ?

CHAMBERLAIN (*secretly*).

He wears away
And perishes in contemplation
Of the bright queen. O woe, woe for China !

2ND TRAVELLER (*secretly*).

All is changed then, if these men lose their masks

M   161

And in their narrow Oriental eyes
Love and fear show so plainly.

PRINCE.

When she speaks,
Like the strange cadences of modal songs,
Her words at once perplex and charm the ear.

(He stops as if choked, and sways on his feet.)

2ND TRAVELLER.

Look to the prince ! Quickly ! The prince is falling !

CHAMBERLAIN.

If with your foreign eyes you'd see the queen,
She walks now in the garden to the lake ;
There you may see her, she in yellow silk.

(The TRAVELLERS run to the corner of the scene to watch.

The PRINCE falls heavily in a swoon.)

CHAMBERLAIN (*bending over him*).

I cannot wake him, but he is not dead.
Send for a doctor quickly !

162

1ST TRAVELLER (*turning back*).

Could you see her?

2ND TRAVELLER.

A moment. She's a wench that's well enough
But yellow as these Chinese women are,
Though not so much as they. She did not smile
But seriously went upon her way,
Holding a fan. What did you see in her?

1ST TRAVELLER:

Nothing, for I am old and my weak eyes
Peered watering down the avenue and ached
And could not yet descry her. I grow old
And can see nothing.

CHAMBERLAIN.

Bring a doctor quickly!
The prince lies yet unstirring in his swoon:
I cannot wake him!

(*As the* TRAVELLERS *run to him and bend over the* PRINCE,
the Curtain falls.)

SECOND ACT

SECOND ACT

The QUEEN'S *Pavilion in the gardens of the palace. The*
QUEEN *is discovered before her mirror.*

QUEEN.

Shall I put almond-blossom in my hair
Or flowers of jasmin? Shall I/tie it up
With yellow silk or white? Ah, petty fool,
What strange and small perplexities are these
And womanish! to please, a senseless thing,
An unexpressioned mirror, night by night,
That nightly shows again my own poor praise
And mocks me in reflexion.
The almond blossoms best where God has sown it :
Yonder beside the sleeping lake it stands,
A bare tree misted over with faint flowers,
And the wind gently taps a loose trail to and fro,
Shaking the perfume free.
How still the time is, yet the air's alive
And all its separate particles aquiver

Work madly on my senses and my veins
Till my blood runs like the spilt quicksilver
Upon the chemist's table, that not rests
But smoothly courses on. O darling flowers !
Is it the springtime moving in my body,
The soft and piercing air that breathes on me,
Is it the sight of young and tender grass,
Creeping across the lawn, that wakes in me
This sweet and poignant restlessness of will ?
The bright tints of the figured silks I wear,
The soft-hued shadows lying in their folds,
Where bird and beast and blossom, strangely worked
In golden threads and silver, are confounded
And lie together in a shining dusk,
These fair and gracious things, these gorgeous toys,
And the living emblems of the happy season
Strike and afflict mine eyes with loveliness.
Would that the day were done and darkness here !
For I have watched through ten full hours of light,
From the pale morning to this coloured time,
And every minute stuffed with sights and sounds,
Odours and shapes that stab the naked sense
With too much beauty and too keen a joy ;
And still the long hours float upon their way,
Large with contentment, rich with happiness,
And in conclusion bring the night with them.

'Now the first shades are stealing on the earth
And weariness upon my limbs and eyes :
Already I can feel the darkness come
With sweet relaxing smells and larger sounds,
That are more gentle, and the gift of sleep. . . .

(*Two* SLAVE-GIRLS *enter*.)

What is your business here ?   I would be private.

1ST SLAVE-GIRL.

Suffer, O shining mistress, that we braid
With tender fingers your long lustrous hair
And knot it in a crown upon your head.
We have been taught by many years and whips
Our duty to a queen and where to place
Deftly her jewels with experienced hands,
How to arrange the falling folds of silk
Upon her breast and how to tie her shoes
And how to paint her eyebrows and her lips
With carmine and dark bistre.
We are long used in these things, we have learnt
With tears and bruises and the steady flow
Of our own warm blood running down our heels
Under the strokes of the house-steward's lash
To know our delicate business. Suffer then

That we may wait on you and tend your beauty,
That's worthy of skill so many tears have bought.

QUEEN.

Ever at dusk two slave-girls wait on me
With speeches thus entreating in their mouths,
Whom still I send away.   Is there no end
To all this store of slaves within the house ?
Are not the last yet come ?   I have no need
Of tiring-maids to deck me.   Mine own hands
Are feat enough to drape my falling silks,
To braid my hair and knot it.
Mine own eyes and my mirror do suffice
To judge where lies the jewel meetliest
And where a blossom.   Tell the steward this :
A slave-girl at my elbow wearies me,
When most my heart desires to be alone.

2ND SLAVE-GIRL.

Have pity on us, for we dare not, lady.
What use are we except to tend a queen
And what man keeps the useless in his home
Save with extremity of evil use ?
If you reject us, we go back again
To curses and the bare, stiff whipping-post,
The anguished stripping off of our thin gowns,

The cruel cord that's tied about our wrists
And the whistling leather falling on our backs,
Until our flesh vies with our smarting eyes
And weeps red tears, as they weep free and clear,
Both bitter salt.

1ST SLAVE-GIRL.

                O mistress, be inclined,
Most lovely lady, to look well on us.
We will be mute when we shall wait on you
And will no more disturb your lonely dreams
Than the light porcelain upon your table
Or the long pin that holds your heavy hair.
We are but things that live to do you service
And wait on beauty.

QUEEN.

               What advantage still
Hope you in serving me ? What liberty
For idleness and wantonness and plays
More full of freedom than your state allows ?

1ST SLAVE-GIRL.

Alas, but we are penned and prisoned now,
Who are so young that every day seems long
And yet is cruel swift in robbing us

171

Of precious years wherefrom a joy is due.
We should have pity from you, who can tell
How freely pity should be given to youth,
Licence our lovers freely to entertain,
Where now a sour, hard steward shuts us up,
Bolts close our doors, watches our lattices
For sheets let down or candles set as signs
To guide our pleasure.

QUEEN.

                        And 'tis thus you'd use me ?
Make me a lucky darkness, a fortunate corner
To hide your paramours ?

1ST SLAVE-GIRL.

                        O, you would feel
Compassion for our state, for you are young
And know how greedily time eats the years
Of unused youth.

2ND SLAVE-GIRL (*secretly*).

                        Too hot, too hot ! Be cold !
You speak new words to her, she hath not loved.

QUEEN.

You know this frenzy, then, which, poets tell,
Perplexes men and women, inflames their blood

To fevers and blushing and their sensible tongues
To utter foolish oaths? I have not loved.
My wits are quiet, I am not distraught,
I reason unperturbed, my cheeks are cool,
I sleep all night in peace, I do not wake
Murmuring a name with tears.

1ST SLAVE-GIRL.

> O are you happy?

QUEEN.

I have so smooth and delicate a life,
I cannot tell. I live from day to day,
So thrilling with a sweet and glad unease
In expectation of to-morrow's gladness,
That all my joy's part pain and want of rest.

2ND SLAVE-GIRL.

But your delight, O lady, when it comes,
Does it stop up your pulses, seal your eyes
Against the passage of the light-winged hours
And fill your heart so that you lose all sense
Of earth and being and the weight of time?
For this is love and to find this we love.

173

QUEEN.

My heart beats faster sometimes but not knocks
Against my side in hasty agony,
Great heavy beats, prolonged and intervalled,
As they say lovers' do.

1ST SLAVE-GIRL.

                  But when our hearts
Burst with a joy we cannot tell from pain,
We know we love indeed.

QUEEN.

                  But what is this ?
To hold debate upon a metaphysic,
A very nothing, smoke of smoke, begotten
By empty heat out of vacuity.
You have too much tricked me with your idle tales :
This is enough, begone. Your flesh is free,
No stripes shall mark it, no blood stain it more
For my ingratitude. Go now in peace ;
Who whips you, he himself shall know the lash,
As the king loves me. Be my word your shield.

1ST SLAVE-GIRL.

Our skill is wasted ; we are useless things.

174

2ND SLAVE-GIRL.

Wasted and worse than useless, for tl
Hath shown offence at us.

1ST SLAVE-GIRL.

We have offended, we are miserable,
Unfit to attend upon so bright a queen,
And all our lore in beauty is quite lost.
We will go hence and creep to hide in shame ;
We are worthy to be whipped and if the steward
Dares not to flog us, we will whip each other
And expiate with self-inflicted blows
Our grave offences.

QUEEN.

             Peace, ye noisy children ;
The air is quiet, all the birds are hushed
And you alone make echo my light walls
With false complaint and crying.

1ST SLAVE-GIRL.

             Look! O look!
The king is walking down the avenue
Wrapped in deep converse with two ancient men.
An almond-petal settles on his beard. . . .

2ND SLAVE-GIRL.

Let us be gone. His frowning wrinkled face
That hath no kinship with our youthful cheeks
Makes me afraid. What would his anger be
If he should find us by the queen refused ?
Let us escape him.

(The KING *enters).*

KING.

Loud and loud and loud
Swell the light voices down the avenue
And greet me coming hither, as though I came
Into a covert full of springtime birds.

QUEEN.

Ah me ungrateful ! I have sent again
Your gifts away.

KING.

Will you be lonely still
And still reject the emblems of a queen ?
Let it be as you wish. You shall be pleasured,
If that all I can give be not to give.
Get you hence, children. *(The* SLAVE-GIRLS *go out.)*
This is my hour of colloquy with you,
Most sweet refreshment when the day is done.

176

I am your slave.

KING.

So still you say,
Which in another I should deem humility
Put on for mocking, but your heart is true.
Happy am I to have so fair a slave,
So wise a servant, whom another king
Would not dare call his queen or come to her
Save with gifts loaded, pain expecting eyes
And heart bowed down for tyranny and stripes.
This day is done,
One of my last, for I draw on in age
And there is nothing that is left of it,
Save traces of the sun about the air,
Unless you approve my deeds and give them savour
With good words and sweet nodding of the head.
Listen! The governor of the Mountain Province,
Who spoiled a poor man's patch of hard-raised millet
For private vengeance, is cast down and shamed.
To-day I judged him in the attentive court,
Took all his honours from him, turned him off,
Free and disgraced.

QUEEN.

O that was kingly done!

KING.

Now he shall earn his bread and know how evil
It is to lose a treasure hardly earned.

QUEEN.

O it is evil to be robbed of all,
Stripped, beaten down. The poor must still be sad;
They lose so much because they have so little
And the thin meal, that would disgust our stomachs,
Is doubly bitter set upon their tables,
Seasoned with doubt and sauced with aching fear.
Tell me, the harbour-master of the port,
Who thieved from the poor fishermen half their catch,
When they brought their salt vessels to his piers,
How has he fared to-day? I much misliked
The stout and prosperous seeming of his face
Against the pinched and pitiful regard
Of his accusers. He were guilty enough
To have ruled so fatly over men so thin.

KING.

I had a paper from the governor
Which weightily set forth his services,
How he has been a lion in our part
To put down smugglers, how he gave the alarm,

Five years gone, when the Indian fleet approached,
Threatening the harbour.

And for this you spared him?

(KING *nods*.)

QUEEN.

What services can outweigh his injustice?
O my dear lord, if he had asked a guerdon
For these his deeds and you had granted it,
When he proceeded : Give me leave to pill
And rob the king's poor subjects, you'd have answered—
What would you have said, my lord? O it is shame
That thus the poor can sweat and suffer still,
Even when the ruler is so wise a man
And my heart sickens when I think of all
The scattered kingdoms of the unhappy earth
Where cruel men and careless boys are crowned.

KING (*after a moment's silence*).

You are just
And in the heat and hurry of your youth,
You follow still unswayed the difficult path

That an old king's feet cannot keep for long
Without your guidance. I will put him down,
As you commanded me. I am ashamed.
I will put him down; there shall be an end of him.
Yet do not think that I to pleasure you
Do justice on my subjects. You have shown me
How glad a thing is justice and how glad
A king's heart is in judging righteously.
I would not that the good deeds of your hand
Should be the like of any concubine's
Boons begged at midnight in the shameful bed.

QUEEN.

They will not say so, who have known your virtue.
You have given me your riches and your love
And I am happy in the much I have.
It is enough for me and I will study
How to repay you with the scanty gifts
That are my own indeed. I will not steal
Any least shred of your benevolent deeds
To deck my queenship with.

KING.

             But all is yours
And I am yours and you are grown my life,
A new blood beating in my ancient pulse.

For there are voices speaking in young blood,
Which an old heart no longer hears. They tell
Of truth and justice and brave work to do.
I do remember when they were my own ;
It is long since. . . .

(*He stands musing.*)

                   I bring you here a gift,
Strange and of value to the curious mind,
Two travellers from the unimagined West,
Who were my guests once and who loved me well,
Which love has brought them hither once again
A perilous journey through the springless waste.
They were my friends and they are very wise,
They have large learning and a store of tales
Fit to delight a queen.

QUEEN.
              It shall be joy
Enough to welcome them if they have loved you.

KING (*going to the door*).
They rest their bodies on a green soft bank
And breathe in quietly the excellent air.
What peace and knowledge rest within their eyes !

The calm sweet memory of a coloured life
Shines in the stirless lids. O they are happy,
Who are not weary save with labour done
And toil accomplished. So may I rest some day
But the end approaches and the goal not yet.
Come, friends. The queen invites you; you may come.

(*The* TRAVELLERS *enter*.)

1ST TRAVELLER.

The love and reverence we bore the king
Is now not halved but doubled for your sake.
Take then our love, O lady, and our prayers
That China still may prosper in your rule.

2ND TRAVELLER.

We are two travellers, whose way has been
Cast in the deserts where no beauty is.
Now a strange gladness falls upon our hearts
Merely to see you.

QUEEN.

                    You have loved my lord
And I accept your love. Halve it or double,
The whole shall go to him; I could not stay
So good a gift from him. Rise, travellers,
For I am hungry for the tales you know.

O, we have come a long and weary way,
Past all your fancy, lower than your dreams,
Through many dangers but most tedious
For you to hear of. Will a list set out
Of all the deserts we have suffered in
Take and rejoice your ears with entertainment,
Gobi and Shamo and the salten waste
Beyond Bokhara and the lonely marshes
That lie beside the desolate Caspian ?
We went on weary feet, bestrode strange beasts,
Were passengers in foul and evil ships
And we are here. We stayed with many kings,
Splendid or barbarous, smooth-tongued or rough ;
In hovels and in palaces alike
We lay awake all night in sweating fear
To feel the treacherous blade that severs throats
Of innocent sleeping men and no word said.
Once in Stamboul we saw a lady die,
A lovely lady who had done no hurt,
Trussed in a sacking like a market-beast
And flung to drown, when dawn with splendour gilt
The bitter choking waters of her death,
Because she loved. And once in Samarcand,
The fabled town, we saw a beggar throned,

Who set the crown upon his greasy head
And gave the law out in a villain's voice
To silken lords, who stooped and kissed his foot,
And in Thibeth we saw the monasteries,
Where the Grand Lama rules his drowsy monks,
Who waste the day with turning of a wheel,
That serves instead of grace and gracious deeds.
How ticklish and alive is memory !
Stir but the brain and the pot boils and bubbles
And steams out pictures of the endless road,
How here we went a day through lofty tops
By tracks and mountain-paths that scare the sense
And over smooth, unfriendly fields of ice
And jutting shelves and cornices of snow
That trembled as we trod, the while the wind
Curling round graven buttresses of rock
Played like an icy lightning in the air
And froze our purposes ; and how we came
Heavily at the end of the afternoon
Over long slopes of short and bitten grass
On to the shoulder of a blowing hill
And saw the dreaming country spread beneath
Under the faint mist and the falling sun
Wrapt in a magic peace. There we have stood
And let our burdens drop and breathed again
The wreathing sweetness of the valley air

That rises warmly from frequented fields
To cheer the naked hills. O we have stood
Silent and felt a singing in our hearts
To see how patient, careful man has made
A garden of his earth.
Here we went sweating up a narrow, stony
Root-cumbered lane between low-arching trees
In crushing darkness that could not conceal·
The steepness of the wooded mountain-side
And there we halted in a shallow glade,
Whose marshy middle the blue gentian decked,
And slept uneasily and woke at dawn
With fever fretting softly at our bones.
·These are the ornaments of voyagers,
This hand a camel crushed in Turkestan,
This limping heel a Tartar's arrow struck,
This bended back with ague hath been doubled
All a long night amid the Volga's reeds ;
But these mine eyes are bright for having seen
Death and escape, murder and treachery
And sunrise in the mists of the high hills.
O in the wide waste world there's much to see
For those who'll buy with danger !
Wonders lie thick as in a raree-show
And the showman is old Death. But we have seen,
Between the wide and the shuttered gates of day

And in the long, slow hours of perilous night,
Twixt Tuscany where too the cherry blows
And your bright country, no town made for rest,
No vale that tempted us to lie in it,
Though dusty were our heads and torn our feet
With the long journey.

KING.

So his epic's done
But briefly, though the end of it be good.

QUEEN.

Old travellers, you are most fortunate,
You have purchased wonders wisely. . . .
I would see other lands and learn how there
The spring arises, how the blossoms grow
Mantling in beauty round the standing trees,
And burn away at last at summer's touch,
Leaving the naked fruit behind. I'd learn
If all men there are happy, ploughing, sowing
Or working stoopt among the golden ears
Or taking the sweet apples from the boughs
And laying them by rows in country lofts
Or striding through the keen winds of the sea.
I have a great wish to go far to-day :

186

My body moves and turns within my silks,
Restlessness and I know not what of fear
Devour me.

KING.

     The sap mounting in the trees
Draws your blood with it, for your blood's like sap,
That goes to feed the topmost flowering bough.

QUEEN.

There is something in me stirring like the sap,
A new sharp ache, a pain I would not lose.
O if I were a man, I'd take a horse
And ride all night with stars to be my guide
And echo for a groom to follow after.
I'd ride all night until the mountains stood
Patient beneath the flying hooves, and on,
Along the causeway through the low, rich lands,
High built and sure, beneath a young May moon
Hung in the heavens, like a new-born moth,
That only now unfolds her velvet wings,
And ride still on and reach the palace gates,
Weary and sated and prepared for rest,
When peasants go out yawning to their fields.
What is this racing madly in my veins ?

187

My eyes hurt me, my breasts hurt me and my hands
For thought of all the loveliness I see.

1ST TRAVELLER.

It is the spring, dear queen.

2ND TRAVELLER (*unheard*).

Perhaps—the spring !

QUEEN.

Call me my groom, my lord, and bid him saddle
My too long stabled horse. Ah, he and I
Alike have suffered in captivity
Where generous spirits turn to acid sour.
Will you call him, my lord, will you allow me
To ride abroad—to-night—unguarded ?

KING.

Ah !

What would you ? But I will not stay your wish
Nor linger in fulfilment.

QUEEN.

Take no heed :

I am foolish and the empty breath of folly

188

Fades in intent as mist on winter days
Blown from the mouth.

KING.

What would you?

QUEEN.

Nothing now,
Save to be rested, to lose count of time
And have in peace dominion of my senses.

KING.

The young have growing pains, which we forget,
But which we'd feel again were't possible.

(*The* CHAMBERLAIN *enters and throws himself at the*
KING'S *feet.*)

CHAMBERLAIN.

Supreme Magnificence of Highest Heaven!
Your son—

QUEEN.

The prince—

KING.

My son?

189

CHAMBERLAIN.

                                My lord, he lies
These eight hours in a still and deathly swoon,
Breathing, not sentient. All the doctor's art
Avails not on his body and he lies
Under the yellow hangings of his bed
With pinched and bloodless face. His creeping pulse
So dimly moves, with such faint finger marks
The passage of his life that scarce the blood
Runs through his slackened limbs. Three doctors watch
    him,
Equally bowed with science and many years,
Who can do nothing. Still the swoon goes on.

                        QUEEN.

O !

                    2ND TRAVELLER (*unheard*).

                            Mark the queen !

                        KING.

                        He is my best-loved son,
And losing him—

                    1ST TRAVELLER.

                        My lord, we saw him fall
And guessed not that his sickness was so heavy
We were even speaking with him.

QUEEN.

Go to him
Quickly and take these learned men to him.
O surely in the desert you have found
Strange herbs and charms our books are ignorant of
And such may save him.

1ST TRAVELLER.

All the skill we have,
All drugs that now do fill our satchels, shall
With our good will attend on his disease
And we'll contrive his health.

QUEEN.

Then go, my lord,
For in such swoons the soul irresolute stands
In the mouth and nostrils, in the doors and portals
Of the warm comfortable body, loth
To leave her fashioned home yet pressed to go,
But will not if the right cure be but found.
Go to him quickly.

(*The Curtain falls.*)

THIRD ACT

THIRD ACT

The Prince's chamber with dimly burning lamps. The PRINCE *lies motionless in a bed which is hung with yellow. Three* OLD DOCTORS *stand watching him.*

1ST DOCTOR.

In my last medicine, in my final charm,
There was no succour. All my essences
A thousand times distilled by cunning slaves
And filtered and refined till every drop
Burns and is bright with the residing power,
All these administered have no effect
Upon his magic and unnatural sleep.

2ND DOCTOR.

Still the pulse changes not.

195

3RD DOCTOR.

When you can feel it,
It beats at the same slow unveering rate,
Such speed as scarce will keep a snake alive,
The slowest breathing of all blooded things.

2ND DOCTOR.

Should we try toads' lungs boiled with cinnamon
And made into a plaster for the breast?
When I was young and daily sought the schools,
Quick rumour said a mighty doctor there,
One of my masters, saved a child with it,
Who lay a week in such a swoon as this,
Though he denied it.

3RD DOCTOR.

Ah, my amulet!
It should have saved him, if I had it now.
It came to me from old Confucius' time
And drove the strongest evils from their seat.
A patient stole it.

1ST DOCTOR.

See him lying there!
Sweet sirops and the sticky juice of fruits,

Fine juice of herbs and the medicinal earths,
Gum arabick compounded with pomegranates,
And sifted dust of powdered chrysoprase,
All I have used and still the trance unshaken
Laughs at my sweating pains.

3RD DOCTOR.

It is a devil,
Which with burnt paper and with holy words
We must expel from him.

2ND DOCTOR.

It is a worm,
Which lodges in a passage of the brain
And there impedes its working.

1ST DOCTOR.

None of these :
If it had been disease or worm or devil,
It should have yielded up to me ere this.
It is no sickness I was taught to meet,
My masters knew not of it.

3RD DOCTOR.

Nor mine either.

2ND DOCTOR.

God grant it may not be the plague again
Come in another shape and deadlier
As it is wont to do.

1ST DOCTOR.

> The plague !

3RD DOCTOR.

> The plague !

1ST DOCTOR.

Put not this shape of evil in our eyes
Which now must float between the light and us
And haunt us. If this thing be true indeed,
We three are doomed to die a dreadful death,
With swelling in our loins and sweating blood
And swollen tongues that stop the dying speech.
When I was young, long ere you two were born,
I saw the plague come down on us. It rose
Out of the northward desert, where no man is
And smote our borders. Then the people lay
Groaning in heaps beside their stinking houses ;
For when a woman perished in a house
Her husband would not come to bury her
But stayed upon the threshold and there died.

Sons brought not water to their sinking fathers ;
In the ungarnished house of government
Rotted unhelped the tainted mandarins.
All, all ! it seemed—my father and my mother !
And there, a child, I straitly vowed my life
To healing and the tending of men's bodies ;
All labour spent in vain, for now a cause
Arises needing my most delicate skill
And finds me wanting. O I am ashamed !

2ND DOCTOR.

No man continues long in this ill posture ;
If the prince wake not now, he dies.

3RD DOCTOR.

And we ?

1ST DOCTOR.

I fear the old king in his grief.

2ND DOCTOR.

And I
Fear for the king. Have you not noticed him,
How he is changed, how all his looks and customs
Are dangerously altered from their wont ?

I have distinguished in him many signs
Of ominous reading. In his age he lives
As though his body were grown young again
And his dry veins were flushed with youthful blood
To wash out the old channels, long disused,
Of vehemence and royal energy.
Our honoured scientists have set it down,
Living a long time closeted with books,
In solitude to water budding thought,
How these things token dangerous maladies
And slow diseases that assail the brain.
He grows as mad as those that waste in prison,
Tearing the straw behind the pitiless bars,
And did no sceptre nor no royal robes
Assure him from their fate, he'd lie with them.

1st Doctor.

The queen has touched the springs of youth in him,
Renewed his wasting sinews, made more supple
His hardening arteries
And breathed a new and an amazing strength
Into his nostrils and his panting lungs.

2nd Doctor.

She is a woman visibly unsound,
Whose passion for defending of the weak

And febrile love of colours and·bright flowers
Proclaim her tainted and degenerate.
The prince himself, who lies there hardly breathing,
Is plainly epileptic, and his case,
Though past the bounds of any practical skill,
Is not beyond the grasp of theory.
We doctors know by reading of much print
What flaws and faults to find in royal houses.

3RD DOCTOR.

Softly ! The king comes and a train with him.

2ND DOCTOR.

Stand round the prince and take his pulse again.

(*The* DOCTORS *go to the bedside and the* 1ST DOCTOR *takes
the* PRINCE'S *wrist. The* KING *enters, followed by the*
TRAVELLERS *and the* CHAMBERLAIN.)

1ST DOCTOR (*solemnly*).

His blood goes slowly as a hill-fed river
In deepest winter when no snow doth melt.

KING.

Put up your drugs, put up your instruments,
O men of little worth ! Is it for this

The state has taught you and has nourished you
So many years till your long beards are grey ?

1st Doctor (*bowing*).

Slay us, O mighty monarch, but delay
Our death a little, for these foreigners
Will surely heal the prince and we'd observe
The unsuspected cure. Why, it is true
That we are men of base and little worth ;
But grant us this, the last request we make,
For we are famished even now for knowledge.
Grant it, great lord ; we would learn one thing more
Before we die.

2nd Doctor (*bowing*).

There is no end to learning
And even in the doorway of the grave,
A man may turn his head to read one line
Before departing.

3rd Doctor (*bowing*).

Let us not go down
To ignorant death and lie unlearned corpses.
For surely still our curious ghosts would walk,
With pens and tablets in their shadowy hands,
To learn this one thing more.

KING.

Be silent, men
Of vanity and flatulent, swollen science,
Whom but to hear is to abhor. Begone !

2ND DOCTOR (*secretly*).

Thank God for it.

1ST DOCTOR.

We will depart, my lord.

(*The three* DOCTORS *bow deeply and go out.*)

KING.

Go to him, friends. My only hope's in you.

1ST TRAVELLER.

I have looked at him, tested his pulse and heart,
Lifted his lids and looked upon his eyes,
And hearkened his scant breath but there's no salve
That ever I have heard of would revive him.
This is a sickness that is strange to me
And I've seen many men die many deaths,
Scurvy and leprosy and the damp ague
That breaks the bones with its strong shivering.
But this is none of these.

KING.

He is alive,
They tell me, though his sleep resembles death.
Is there no man can help him and help me ?
The new-born power, so gracious in my hands,
Runs through my fingers now like falling water
And I am helpless. Why, a king can kill
With any sort of death, but when he stands
At the sad bedside of his dying son,
He is as powerless as another man.

CHAMBERLAIN.

O woe, woe, woe on China ! Now is all
The fabric of the high-arched kingdom gone
And the fair provinces, the Mountain Province,
The Province of the Plain, the River Province,
The Border Countries and the teeming port
And cities where the wise old Viceroys rule,
Shaking their honoured governmental heads,
All these are wounded. O he is a prince
That is a paragon of youthful virtues
And is fulfilled of unexampled good !

KING.

Had I not kingly state and governance,
I'd rave as he does.

CHAMBERLAIN.

Is there nought indeed?
Can you not save him?

1ST TRAVELLER.

He's in the hands of God.
And hangs suspended by a viewless chain
High out of our perception.

CHAMBERLAIN.

I've a plan,
If but the king will hear me.

KING.

Speak, old servant.

CHAMBERLAIN.

With these poor doctors we've not used up yet
The treasures of the wisdom of the realm.
In a corner of the royal library,
Hidden by books heaped like a monument,
Sits an old sage, old beyond reckoning,
To whom I am a child. He studies there
And studied there when you and I were young,
Distilling all the toil of his long life,

205

All honey gathered from his dusty flowers,
To make one page in the great dictionary.
Who knows what he has found in such a time,
Strange remedies in unaccustomed script
And charms by us forgotten ?

KING.

Seek him out :
This is a spider's thread of slender hope
And yet no worse than nothing. Seek him out.

CHAMBERLAIN.

I go, O majesty.

(*He goes out.*)

1ST TRAVELLER.

Take courage, sir ;
Still the prince lives.

KING.

He lives still, yes, I know,
And set some hope thereon. But is it life,
In which the blood forgets its usual custom
And slides as slowly as a glacier,
Which once ran rapid as a hill-side stream ?
His veins are new and fresh, he is a youth,

Whose body is a playground for the blood
To run and leap in. Were it in my veins
That this sad stoppage held its dreadful sway,
I could not marvel but I marvel now
And weeping in wondering.

1ST TRAVELLER.

O we weep with you,
Tears of suspense, my lord, but not of loss,
For nothing is yet lost while he's alive.
And this old sage, whose coming we attend,
May have recovered something from the waste
Of hungry years,
As we have found bright gold in desert sands.
And if he aid not, there is nature yet,
Always our last hope in the deepest ills.

KING.

Here in my land we put no trust in her,
Save when our learned men have wrestled with her
And got good gifts by force.

2ND TRAVELLER.

The Chamberlain
Comes hasting back and brings with him a man,
As old as China.

(*The* CHAMBERLAIN *comes in, followed by an* OLD SCHOLAR.)

CHAMBERLAIN (*to the* KING).

                    Pardon, lord ; his wisdom
Hath clogged his brain and made him mannerless.
Be merciful to his old rusted wits,
Whereon the dust of many books hath settled,
And hear him out in patience.

KING.

               Let him speak.

OLD SCHOLAR.

I knew your grandfather and you are like him
But he was taller and less pouched at the eyes
And had a nobler carriage of the head.
Where is he now ?

KING.

                  He is a long time dead
My father too is dead and I am king.

OLD SCHOLAR.

What ! dead so young ? O it is pity, pity !
And boys must rule the state with their rash hearts
And hands by age unpractised. We, the old,

Love not this quick and youthful governance,
Knowing how years bring wisdom.

CHAMBERLAIN.,
There's the Prince,
Lying there ghastly on the yellow bed.
See to him quickly, if speed be in your limbs,
And use what wisdom the long years have given.

(*The* OLD SCHOLAR *goes to the* PRINCE *and examines him,
while a deep silence fills the room.*)

OLD SCHOLAR.

He is well and strong but in a powerful trance
And so may live while all of us decay.
Your grandson's grandsons may discover him,
When we are all forgotten, sleeping still,
Unchanged and uncorrupted.

KING.

Thus to live !
Must China then be ruled by a sleeping king ?
Better that he should die, for while he lives
No other of my sons may mount the throne.
I swore it in the temple five years gone,

Feasting my birthday with the Ancestors ;
They heard and noted down my pious vow,
Nodding their wise and ghostly heads for sanction.
That was the oath I swore. May I . . . should I . . .
Take in my hands the crime and on my head
The guilt—the guilt—the guilt—

OLD SCHOLAR.

                    Be quiet, man.
You dam the flow of wisdom and bar up
With your intemperate, youthful vehemence,
My loaded words. This illness came on him
By human causing. Neither drug nor blow
Assailed the prince nor any dark disease.
He is wounded, though ye see no welling blood
Nor any open gash. The wound lies deep
Upon the delicate fabric of the soul
And stops his being up. But there's a cure :
Search out the spirit that thus has wrought on his.
The soul alone which did this can undo.

KING.

But who's the man ? Who'd wish to harm my son
Or hurt him with a spell, a sword-blade forged
Of whispered words and dark imaginings ?

He is not hated ; even in his sickness,
His words were courteous and his looks were kind.
Who is the murderer ?

OLD SCHOLAR.

No murder this !
Full well I know how mind can shatter mind
With airy weight and blows. You walk your ways,
Slaying in blindest ignorance with a thought
And maiming with desires. O foolish men !
Who are most like to children armed with daggers
Or playing with huge poisons. Learn of my wisdom,
Poor wisdom ! that still makes a crutch for fools
And may not walk alone. I bid you now
Seek out the prince's servants and his friends,
All that are daily round him, all that touch
His life materially with passing hands
Or with the frailest woven web of thought.
Then let them walk beside him as he lies
And touch him, each one gently on the brow ;
The right man's touch will call him back to life.
Let what I bid be done. Farewell !

(*He goes out.*)

CHAMBERLAIN.

He is gone

211

KING.

Let what he bids be done. It is a chance
Built up too high and slender in the fancy
To bear the weight of any useful hope,
Yet we will try it.

1st Traveller.

Call the prince's servants !

KING.

Stay !

CHAMBERLAIN.

Ah, my lord—

KING.

I faint, my will gives way,
I cannot see it. O put off the test.
Hope grows, a wretched seedling in my heart,
With pale and sapless leaves and drooping stem ;
Let me a moment nourish it. Let me—

2nd Traveller.

Hold him, he shakes—

1st Traveller.

Your hand behind his shoulders,
So !—

KING.

I am better. Look not thus with fear
On age's and on grief's infirmity.
Give me a moment. I can breathe again.
O, how it caught my heart.

1ST TRAVELLER.

      We'll lead you hence
Into your own apartments and with you
Await the outcome of the trial.

KING.

    No !
I will not go so far, I'll stay with him
And sooner learn if there be any hope.

2ND TRAVELLER.

Wait till the morning's light.

KING.

     I could not sleep
And could not watch all night and nothing done.
Give me a moment. I am better now.
The thing shall now be done.

CHAMBERLAIN.

We'll draw the curtain
That shuts the alcove off. You shall not see
The long procession going by and by
Or watch with sick hope and o'erstrainèd heart
Each hand raised up to touch him.

(*He draws a curtain hiding the bed.*)

I will go
And set the train in motion. As the first
Go by his bed, I'll marshal up the rest
And send swift messengers about the city
To fetch his noble friends.

(*He goes out.*)

2ND TRAVELLER.

We'll not despair,
While anything is doing. Sit, my lord;
Shall we with coloured travellers' tales beguile you?

KING.

To-day I have been happy as a youth
For all the toils of kingship had grown light
And turned to toys which I manipulated

214

With easy fingers. Now here is a woe
Beyond the great new wisdom I have learnt.
It passes me : I am too old a man.

But not so old as I nor yet so worn
With dangers.

KING.

Surely that step was the first !
There goes another and another now.

(*The* CHAMBERLAIN *comes in.*)

CHAMBERLAIN.

I have set the court in motion now and all
Pass in an anxious stream beside the bed
For any commoner may have the touch
Of curing sickness, formerly reserved
For kings alone.

KING.

Stay with us now, old friend.
I need all my old friends now.

1st TRAVELLER.
We are here.

215

KING.

I'll not forget it.

CHAMBERLAIN (*after a pause*).

Still the train goes on,
Guards, waiting-maids, the servants of the bath,
Gardeners, grooms and all the varletry
That fills the court.

1ST TRAVELLER.

But still as it goes on
Hope lingers. Till the last poor slave has been
We'll not despair of him.

2ND TRAVELLER.

Still they go on
And still I hear the sound of those to come.

(*The Curtain falls.*)

SCENE TWO.

The same, not long before the dawn, with the curtain still hiding the Prince's bed. The KING, *the two* TRAVELLERS *and the* CHAMBERLAIN *sit round a small brazier, in which charcoal is burning.*

216

How all night long my flesh has crawled to hear
The shuffling and the laughter going by,
The steady tramp of the insensate feet
Of the poor slaves, who came to try their touch
And in mechanical procession tread
Our last and fading hopes to dust.
How they have laughed and nudged and clasped at hands
And pulled at garments and gone breathless by,
The idiots, to whom anything that's strange
Makes an occasion for a holiday.
What cookmaid was it that went by just now,
With greasy clothes and breath of very kitchen
And harsh loud piercing whisper, out of sight?
Was she the last to go?

                  The last has gone
Two hours back in the dead and depth of night.

Two hours gone! but a sound—just here—just now—
Under my head, in the very gate of my ear,
That hath stood strained all night—
The last wave of that hideous flowing tide

That beat in loud succession on the shore,
What was the sound, friend, tell me—

1ST TRAVELLER.

You have slept
More than two hours and we have watched alone,
The Chamberlain and I, in misery,
Warming our hands above this charcoal fire,
Stretching our palms out to the flameless glow,
Of use and custom, not for comfort's sake.
Awake and share our vigil; we have dreamt
The long night through with still unclosing eyes,
While the dark skies encompassed us around
With walls of blackness that closed in on us
And choked our breath. We dreamt in solitude
Of endless evil striking like a sword
Upon the land of fertile happiness,
Of sickness eating like a minute worm,
The fruit's sweet centre.

2ND TRAVELLER.

Is the king asleep?

CHAMBERLAIN.

His eyes are closed, his head has fallen back,

218

His hands rest still upon the chair's curved arms,
His body lies relaxed—he is asleep.

1st Traveller.

Hush, hush ! He does not sleep, but his great age
Makes nature kindly to his brain. He lies
Wrapt in a stupor of the o'erwrought soul,
Which now is drugged from pain by pain itself.
Thus sorrow floods out sorrow and the evil
Defeats its own damned armies.

King.

It is gone,

That weary caravan of dwindling hope.

1st Traveller.

The night is not yet gone and you are weary.
Lay back your head upon the pillow there
And sleep awhile.

King.

O, I am fain of sleep.

(*He lies back again and sleeps.*)

2nd Traveller.

What's to be done now ?

219

1st Traveller.

                    Let the dead king sleep,
Beside his son that is alive in death,
For there is nothing left. All stratagems,
Devices and procurings of the wise
Are shown as empty and as useless things,
As dances of the desert dervish-doctors,
Who mock the sick with leaps and attitudes,
Which we have mocked at. There is nothing left,
Save to expect the coming of the day
And ruin with it.

Chamberlain.

                    Still the day comes on ;
The fountain now stands out all silvery clear,
That through the sad hours beat upon my brain
With dull recurrence of its falling drops.

2nd Traveller.

Did you not say the land slept on unchanged ?

Chamberlain.

All was the same—and still the country sleeps
In comfort unawakened till this day,
Which I prevent not, which I will not flee,
Which shall enwrap us with its dawning fear,

As we sit still and wait on its approach.
But what shall be thereafter well I know
And what the evils falling on the state.
In a few years this country shall decay,
Our joyous houses and our porcelain towers
Shall be thrown down and all the garden-walks
Be choked with darnel and the hungry thistle
And barren weeds that turn the land to waste.
The enemy shall cast us down and rise
In hideous triumph on our fallen bodies :
The capital shall be deserted, yea,
The planks of the thronged wharves shall warp and start,
Strange river-snails crawl over them, the worms
That in the river's bottom have their home
Shall eat with puny teeth the seasoned baulks
And bring the whole to ruin.   The canals,
Placid and level, only now disturbed
By passage of our wealthy merchandise,
Shall be stopped up with growth of water-weed
And spread their sluggish floods among the crops.
The royal roads shall pit and rut and break
With softening rain and the disrupting frost.
Yea, even the goldfish in the garden-court
Shall weep this day,
For when our city's fired, their bowl will crack
And 'eave them to be choked in bitter air.

2ND TRAVELLER.

Must all the people slumber with the prince
Nor wake at any call to know these wrongs ?

CHAMBERLAIN.

You know not how we are ringed with enemies

1ST TRAVELLER.

Soften your voices. Leave the king to sleep,
Till the full sun is risen on the earth.
There is miraculous healing in the light
For broken spirits, there's no cordial
For grief that can be likened to the sun,
No cloak beneath which sorrow festers more
Than darkness and there is no poison known,
That worse can rankle in the spiritual wound,
Than this grey merciless light of early dawn.

CHAMBERLAIN.

The king sleeps well. Would that I too could sleep
And find forgetfulness of misery.

2ND TRAVELLER.

But he is sicker than his helpless son.
See how the bright eyes through the wearing lid

Shine out with fever, how his wasting hands
Grow thinner, whiter. He is close to death.
O fetch the doctors for him !

CHAMBERLAIN.

They have fled,
Fearing his wrath most foolishly.

2ND TRAVELLER.

Alas !
For the wise men whose wisdom fails them now.
How are we better ?

1ST TRAVELLER.

Soft ! the king awakes !

KING.

I have slept long and still mine eyes are heavy ;
You should have waked me, I have slept too long.

1ST TRAVELLER.

You have slept ten minutes, sire. Lie down again
For you are weary and in need of rest
And we will wake you at a better time.

KING.

I have slept too long already. Now I know
Why I am weary. Is the last one gone?

CHAMBERLAIN.

The last has gone and left no hope behind.

KING.

And my son sleeps yet? Has not once he stirred?

1ST TRAVELLER.

His breathing has not altered through the night,
Not even in the dim and dreadful hour,
When the waking are most sad and the sick oft die.

KING.

Send for that ancient man again. I'll ask him
If he has used up all his armoury
Of quaint extravagant devices now.
Strange that we do expect beneath the veil
Of rustic mannerlessness in learned men
A more than common wisdom.

1ST TRAVELLER.

Let him sleep, sire,

224

And you too sleep. There is no profit now
In waking.

KING.

                       I will see him, I will ask him
What he can do—whether he— Send for him !

2ND TRAVELLER.

Let it all rest, my lord, I do implore you,
Till there's warm light to see by.

KING (*as if dazed or in a dream*).

                  Send for him !
I am told to ask you for him.

(*The* 1ST TRAVELLER *makes a sign that the* KING *is to be
obeyed.*)

CHAMBERLAIN.

                I will bring him.
He rises early and is with his books
By the first light. I'll bring him to you soon.

(*He goes out.*)

1ST TRAVELLER.

Give me your hands, sir. They are cold and I
Will warm them twixt my palms.

KING.

I am all cold
And neither sunshine nor the bright coal-fire
Nor human blood can warm my limbs again,
For the chill spreads outward, moving from the heart.

(*The* CHAMBERLAIN *comes in, followed by the* OLD SCHOLAR.)

KING (*listlessly*).

Are you so old that you have done with sleep,
To be thus early playing with your books?

OLD SCHOLAR.

Why have you sent for me?

KING.

You have cured my son,
Have you not cured him? Go and look at him,
How the sweet sleep of health doth wrap him up
And sooth his body.

1ST TRAVELLER (*secretly*).

This is too much pain
And we are tightened even to cracking point.
(*Aloud.*) Observe your patient, old and learned doctor,

On whom your fine device has fallen as light
As snow on water. Stay among your pens !
You have held us all a night with foolish hopes
And cloaked our brains in fancy till the dawn
With cold and pitiless finger pointed at us
For fools in the light's eyes and in our own.

OLD SCHOLAR.

Is the Prince dead ?

1ST TRAVELLER.

                    He sleeps and sleeps and sleeps
Untouched by your contrivings.

OLD SCHOLAR.

                    This is strange !
I am amazed. My science is not vain :
I have not duped myself with lying arts
And transient, to gather empty praise.

KING.

The King dismisses you ; stay here no longer.
I might have racked you but I have no will
To add to the world's sum of pain.

Old Scholar.

Softly, my friend ; I am no charlatan.
Have you observed with order what I bade you ?
Have all passed by him and laid hands on him ?

Chamberlain.

All have gone by and played the sorry part.
The slaves infect the chamber with their breath
Of kitchens hot and the rank stable-smells
To no avail.

Old Scholar.

       Have all his friends gone by ?

1st Traveller.

Even we, we four, when waiting grew too long,
To break the night, made spaces in the file
And touched his head ourselves and left him sleeping.

Old Scholar.

Have all the women passed ?

2nd Traveller (*sharply but secretly*).

       Unlucky word !

1ST TRAVELLER.

The youngest slave that crouches at the spit
Has touched the Prince.

OLD SCHOLAR.

Has the Queen been here?

(There is a dead silence.)

KING.

Who speaks of the Queen?

CHAMBERLAIN.

He said, sire—

KING.

What, the Queen?
Last farcical and pitiful invention
To play his mummery out with. Idle sir,
Will you pursue your drollery to the end?
Have you no drug, no novel incantation
To play a change with?

OLD SCHOLAR.

I have said my word.

2ND TRAVELLER.

Dismiss this fool, sire.

KING.

Shall we play it out?
There's all the morning to be travelled through
And nought to do in it. We'll fetch the Queen
If this impostor will be satisfied.
She lies in the pavilion by the lake
And does not rise until the day's more up.

(He goes to the window.)

2ND TRAVELLER (*to the* CHAMBERLAIN).

You guessed! You too!

CHAMBERLAIN (*to the* 2ND TRAVELLER).

I would not think of it,
But now it's on us.

2ND TRAVELLER.

What shall we do now?

CHAMBERLAIN.

Blow blindly on like gnats before a storm.
There's nothing else.

KING.

See, still the light is yellow in her windows,
A sallow radiance against the dawn,
That tells of guttering candles. Go to her.

(*The* CHAMBERLAIN *bows and goes out.*)

2ND TRAVELLER (*secretly*).

Old man, you cannot guess what you have said !
Unsay your foolish word and bring him back,
Else equally our happiness is lost
And China ruined. O, a hate begun
Between a king and his succeeding heir
Hath more of evil in it than the plague
That feeds on life.

OLD SCHOLAR.

My science is not vain,
As you have vainly said. Let hate begin
And wreck the land and pull the people down !
I have seen five kings on whom the kingdom hung
By a parting thread and still we live in peace.
What is your kingdom ? what your government ?
I see you from my height of ancient knowledge
Like ants acrawl, as busy and as vain.
Men without learning are even as the ants,

231

Who heap a mighty commonwealth of dust,
Bridging great rivers, tunnelling great hills
And cutting down enormous blades of grass.
They are purposeless and leave no mark behind.

1ST TRAVELLER.

The Queen is coming, sir, and still she wears
The silks of yesterday.

2ND TRAVELLER (*secretly*).

                      True-founded fears !
Now for the storm.

(*The* QUEEN *and the* CHAMBERLAIN *come in.*)

QUEEN.

                     My lord, what must I do ?
Long waking has so worn my heavy eyes,
That in this ghostly and uncertain light
I scarce can see.

KING.

                    O you must touch him, lady.
Learning this most fantastic cure devises
And learning is our master. This old man
Conceives my son to bear a mental wound,

232

Which nothing but a magic touch may heal
And that touch in the wounding hand resides.
Since by light chance you may have wounded him—
So learning's logic goes—do me this service :
Go in and touch him.

QUEEN.

                    Is it nothing more
But only this ? My hands are yours alone,
Should you desire them severed at the wrists.
Lead me on, chamberlain, where I must go.

(*The* CHAMBERLAIN *leads her behind the curtain.*)

OLD SCHOLAR.

The Prince himself shall tell me he is cured ;
Send him to me for I have much to do.

(*He goes out.*)

1ST TRAVELLER.

Now bends she above him, as a branch of blossoms
At sweet compulsion bends, in a lovely curve.

(*There is a dead silence.*)
233

PRINCE (*behind the curtain*).

Pull down those flowers that brush upon my face
And make a garland of them for my head ;
The gods are kindly to the garlanded
And love not them that walk with undecked brow.

1ST TRAVELLER.

He wakes ! He speaks ! What—

KING.

Draw the curtain back !

(*The* 2ND TRAVELLER *throws back the curtain. The*
PRINCE *is seen, half sitting up, drawing the* QUEEN *uncertainly towards him, as though still in a dream.*)

PRINCE.

Have I been sleeping ? All night long I dreamed
That flowers drooped on me and your face among them.
I feel so light, so light, my heart assuaged
That ached and smarted. My limbs feel so free !
Give me your hands again.

KING.

My son ! My son !

Take her away from him ! Ah, this is madness !
My lord, the trance hath worked upon his brain
And his slow-moving and infected blood
Bears along poisonous fancies in its flow.
My lord, it is the sickness still that sways.

2ND TRAVELLER (*muttering*).

You know it is not.

KING.

Ah, my son ! my son !

QUEEN (*softly, near weeping*).

Unclasp his hands and give him cordial :
The quickening liquor shall bring back his wits.
Unclasp his fingers, chamberlain. You see
How tightly they have closed upon my gown
So that I cannot get away from him.
I have done my part now ; let the doctors come,
Who shall restore him.

PRINCE (*fully awake*).

What am I dreaming now ?
What am I clasping ? Is it you indeed ?
And is all ended that deep-scored my heart,

A hundred harrow-points in every day,
That caught and tore the tender fibres up,
Each time I saw you ? Do not leave me now,
I am hardly cured, hardly aware of health,
That yet is entering the open sluices
And filling up my body.

QUEEN (*struggling*).

Let me go !
The King is here.

KING (*to* 1ST TRAVELLER).

Give me your hand, good friend,
And help me from the place. I'll leave them here.
There is another room not far from this,
Where sometimes in the morning I have sat
And counted breaking buds upon the limes.
I can just go so far. I'll lean on you.

PRINCE.

O love, my throat and utterance are choked up,
My heart rejects its business. Speak for me
And tell me of the love between us two,
So long time nourished secretly.

236

QUEEN (*weeping*).

My love !

(*She goes into his arms.*)

KING.

It is done. They see no more of us, no more.
Our place is not within the bridal-chamber,
Whence ancient men and foolish are shut out.
Take me hence, friends.

1ST TRAVELLER.

　　　　　　　Sir, you must speak to them
And cheer them ere you go, lest they imagine
Vain shapes of royal wrath and shameful death.
That kings' wives know of and their paramours.

KING.

O this is hard to do. My son ! My son !

PRINCE.

Father, are you too here ? O, I am joyful
That you have read my secret and confirmed
By this last seal the happiness you give me.
Is she not fair ? I am struck by wonder at her
And cannot speak.

237

KING.

My son, I give you her ;
Love her as I do and it is enough.
My queen, a last time you shall be my queen
And sit beside me at the audience,
Which, many years after that I am dead,
Again you'll grace as queen, though then not mine.
Much is to do to-day. The audience
Is packed with business of a weighty sort,
Your marriage first and then the declaration
Of war against the Tartars, which shall be
The last act of my reign. Old Chamberlain,
Send for the general, who counselled me
A war of mighty scope and purposes.
Together we will plan it and together
We'll head the armies. But the marriage first !
Good luck's with us, this is the time of flowers
And flowers shall deck the bridal. Lead, my queen ;
Your prince shall follow.

(*He takes the* QUEEN *by the hand and conducts her to the door. She goes out, while he remains in the doorway.*)

KING.

For the old, old men,
There's nothing and the young are heirs of all.

O it is bitter for an ancient man,
Who sees the years dissolve like smoke before him
And nothing through them but the unfriendly grave,
To know his last delight deserts his side,
His last fool's hope of youthfulness in eld.
Each disappointment that we know in youth
Is wrapped up by the tale of years to spend
And hurts us not, but now the years peel off
And naked sorrow stands before mine eyes
Without a hope to hide her ugliness.
Come with me, friends.

(*He leads out the* TRAVELLERS *and the* CHAMBERLAIN. *The*
PRINCE *sits up in bed, rubbing his eyes. His* SERVANT *enters.*)

SERVANT.

The bath is ready, sir.
The waters, wherein pleasant scents do swim,
Await your body.

PRINCE (*leaping out of bed*).

I am coming to it.
Set out my robes, that there be no delay :
I feel already what short time's a day.

(*They go out in different directions and the stage is left
empty. A* GIRL'S VOICE *is heard singing outside.*)

SONG.

The spring will soon be over,
　The withered flowers are falling,
The crops are growing higher
　And harsh the cuckoo's calling,
But when the spring is over,
I still shall have my lover.

For the spring is but a season
　And love is a delight
That knows not age nor waning
　And hath an endless might,
And when the spring is over
I still shall have my lover.

(The Curtain falls.)

PRINTED BY WILLIAM BRENDON AND SON, LTD.
PLYMOUTH, ENGLAND